A Supersonic Day

From the Packsack of
Gregory Clark

A
Supersonic
Day

Selected and Edited
by Hugh Shaw

McCLELLAND AND STEWART

The Canadian Publishers
McClelland and Stewart Limited
25 Hollinger Road
Toronto M4B 3G2

CANADIAN CATALOGUING IN PUBLICATION DATA

Clark, Gregory, 1892-1977.
  A supersonic day

Selections from the author's newspaper column
"Gregory Clark's Packsack".

ISBN 0-7710-2112-7

I. Shaw, Hugh.   II. Title.

PS8505.L32S97   C818'.5208   C80-094383-X
PR9199.3.C52S97

The publisher would like to thank Louis
Jaques, and the family and friends of Gregory
Clark for the photographs which illustrate the
text, and to express our gratitude to Gregory
Clark, Jr. for making available to us his family
albums.

PRINTED AND BOUND IN THE UNITED STATES OF AMERICA

Contents

Editor's Note

This is the fourth volume of selections from Gregory Clark's Packsacks. The first, *Outdoors with Gregory Clark*, was published in 1971. *Grandma Preferred Steak* was released in 1974, and *Things that Go Squeak in the Night* in 1976.

This volume is the first to be published since Gregory Clark's death. The manuscript had not been completed when he died (on February 3, 1977, at the age of eighty-four), but we had discussed it and had agreed, late in 1976, that we would follow the same method of selection of material for future volumes as was used for the earlier Packsack books. This is not, therefore, in any significant sense a posthumous work.

Here, then, is a new collection of Packsack pieces, offered not as an epitaph but as a sampler of the lasting vigour of Greg Clark's newspaper writing, prepared and dispatched sometimes a day, sometimes only hours, before deadline — with scarcely ever a thought for posterity, a word and a subject he would have found too stuffy for serious consideration.

Hugh Shaw

A Supersonic Day

Blue Dan, a Nipigon Indian guide in whom I place great faith, used the word supersonic. "It is," he stated, "a supersonic day for fishing." I asked him what the word meant:

"I don't know," admitted Blue Dan. "I read it in a newspaper. It is a beautiful word."

"Supersonic," I then explained, "means faster than sound." This puzzled Blue Dan.

"Why," he asked, "do you want a word meaning faster than sound when all you have to say is faster than sound? Aren't there enough words already?"

This naturally led to an enlightening discussion on airplanes and rockets. The whole of white civilization, I informed Blue Dan, now possessed aircraft and rockets that were supersonic – that is, faster than sound can travel.

"Why?" asked Blue Dan.

"It is part of a great program," I explained, "for the improvement of the human race."

"How will it improve them," he enquired, "if they get supersonic?"

"Don't you see?" I cried. "We will be able to get improvements to them so fast, they won't even be able to hear them coming. In fact, they won't even know they are improved."

Blue Dan studied me earnestly for a moment, and then slowly bared his teeth in a genuine Ojibway grin.

"I bet you don't know," he said, "what you mean either. I often think you white people don't know what anything means."

He began to scrub out the frying pan with a wad of newspaper. He suddenly paused, held the wad of paper up before his eyes, and pretended to be engrossed in the type he could see, all smeared with bacon grease.

"Words!" he chuckled. "Words! I am glad I am an Indian."

"Dan," I said, rising from the campfire, "it's a supersonic day for fishing."

The Handicapper

I regret to report that two friends of mine of respectable age and previous good character got into a fist fight. In the life of most of us, I suppose, there comes a time when argument ends and fisticuffs begin. These two have known each other and quarrelled for forty years. Quarrelled over business, over politics, over family affairs. Any number of times I have watched them swell up to the bursting point with anger at each other. They have even clenched fists, even threatened to bop one another on the nose.

A few evenings ago, as the result of a quarrel over a minor incident on last year's hunting trip, on which the younger and larger of the two is alleged to have shot a deer that was coming directly to the older and smaller sportsman, their tempers flared up. I think it must be the autumn that makes men belligerent. The younger and larger man suddenly punched his friend right on the nose.

What happened very immediately thereafter was that the

older and smaller man, thirty pounds smaller, kicked his larger friend on the shin.

The larger friend instantly bent over in pain, thus reducing his height to suitable proportions for the smaller man, to give him a knee in the chin, and the younger and much huskier gentleman went over ignominiously on his back on the drawing-room rug while the older and wirier gentleman danced around him, daring him to get up.

At this point, members of both families came running from all parts of the house and intervened. When they were seated in easy chairs in their opposite corners of the drawing-room, glaring furiously at each other, I arrived on the scene. (We were to have a pre-hunting trip gathering, to make plans.) I was appealed to by the larger and younger man. Had I ever heard of a more dastardly act than kicking an opponent on the shin, doubling him over and then giving him a knee in the chin?

"Who struck the first blow?" I enquired.

It was admitted the younger and larger man had, though with extreme provocation.

My decision was that the Marquis of Queensberry rules were promptly abrogated by the younger and larger man hitting the older and smaller man first. The rules of fair fighting refer only to matched fighters. A large young man takes his life in his hands when he assaults a small old man. He has thrown out the rules to begin with. Thereafter, his opponent may use any tactics, such as chairs, golf clubs, bridge lamps, kicking, gouging, or any other of the methods that come instinctively to mind when one is engaged in fisticuffs.

So they accepted my judgement and shook hands. But I bet it will be an interesting hunting trip this year.

Difficult Days in March

About the twelfth of March each year my family sends our radio set off to the repair shop for its annual overhaul and tune-up. We like them to keep the radio about a week. We want the week of the seventeenth of March to get well by before it comes back.

Unlike St. Andrew or St. George or St. David, St. Patrick is not content with a mere one-day stand. His partisans start whooping it up around the twelfth of March. And if there is one thing we can't bear in our house, it is Irish tenors. The legend in the family is that the reason we quit Ireland in 1818 wasn't on account of the collapse at the end of the Napoleonic Wars, nor the famine, nor the shooting from behind hedges nor the shillelaghs nor the poteen. No, it was just that we couldn't stand Irish tenors any longer. We just gave a hell of a yell, as the saying is, and fled to Canada. And until the radio was invented, we lived happily ever after. We married Scotch people over here, and that was all right, because we only had to put up with the bagpipes one day a year, or at the most two, counting Robbie Burns. We married English people, and maybe we had one day Pomp and Circumstance, and the roses were nice. We married Welsh and had to wear leeks for a day; but we are fond of onions in any form.

But we carefully avoided any further marriage with the Irish, because you never can tell when a tenor will turn up and start singing that he met her in the garden where the praties grow. We eat praties, of course, but prefer them French fried.

Privately, and provided no Irish tenors are within hearing, we are intensely proud of the Irish blood, and go back to dream in Ireland whenever the chance and the purse allow. Some of us were back for the Sixteen, and it wasn't with the Black and Tans. Not only do we wear the shamrock, but we

14

grow it on our window-sills, and George Russell and Yeats and Synge have the place of honour on our shelves.

But by the holy, when the twelfth of March comes, the heck out of here goes the radio.

Discrimination Against Prejudice

One of the chief difficulties with the campaign against racial and religious discrimination is probably the use of the word discrimination. We should hunt for a better one.

Because discrimination is a process we are going through, every hour of the day, every year of our lives. We are discriminating between what we like and what we don't like at every turn. Discrimination between good and bad is the very foundation of our moral code.

Social discrimination goes on at every level of the community, including those who complain most vehemently against racial and religious discrimination. Every one of us has the bars up, every hour of our lives, against certain people and even certain classes of people. Good-living men and women are iron in their determination to have no dealings whatever with loose-livers; and if there is anything more wholehearted than the discrimination practised by rowdies against the prim and teetotal, name it if you can.

We discriminate among our very friends and relations, courting some, and avoiding others like poison. We do not eat, drink, dress, shop, walk ten feet or sit down in a chair without exercising the power of discrimination, choosing one thing and rejecting another. Discrimination might be the first, the elementary process by which we live.

In the racial and religious field, what is really complained of is the prejudice which results in discrimination. And that is a horse of a different colour. To demand that a man or woman cease discriminating without first doing something about the removal of the prejudice is a shotgun business. It can never do anything but aggravate the prejudice, even if it drives it under cover. There is no substitute for understanding.

⟿⊛⟿

A Cheer for Last

In the regatta I attended a year ago, the race that excited me most was the mixed swimming event for five and under. This race was held on a sand beach in about two feet of water. There were seven contestants, five girls and two boys, a rather interesting statistic. Do girls swim at an earlier age than boys? The way the race was run, there was a judge for each contestant. In other words, the judges waded in, each carrying a contestant. They lowered the contestants into the shallow water. And at the word Go, each judge let go of his charge, and the race began. The distance, ten yards.

A more exciting race I never witnessed. Each judge, of course, had to watch the performance of his own particular charge, not only for reasons of safety, but to be able to swear, in the seven-judge consultation after the race, that his charge did not touch bottom while swimming.

Of course there was bound to arise a certain rivalry among the judges. They made quite a sight, floundering along knee-deep behind their diminutive charges and urging them on most mightily. They had to serve as both judges and coaches, which is quite a test of a judge's integrity.

Anyway, the race was a wonderful success. Like the Supreme Court itself, the seven judges arrived at a most just and equitable decision.

The little girl on whom I had put my money came last.

There were only three prizes; first, second, third. And what broke my heart, after so splendid an athletic exhibition was the grief of that little girl on whom I put my money. To be last was bad enough. But to get no prize was devastating.

It then occurred to me that we do everything wrong in this life. Is it not enough to be first? Is it not enough, indeed, to come second or even third? Is there nothing, then, in honour? Prizes, I think, should be given to those who fail. Prizes should all be consolations to those who, perchance, are beautiful and five years or under, and full of a furious if misdirected energy. Indeed, the girl I had my money on went in all directions.

This year's regatta, I got a pretty little Chinese wind chime, bits of glass to tinkle from the ceiling of the verandah. And this I gave for the little girl who came last in the race for five and under.

The little girl I had my money on last year, alas, had to move up to the under seven class. But a very proud young lady nonetheless won it. She came last because she didn't go at all. She just floated.

Knots

When a tailor measures you for a suit, there is a strict professional routine to each measurement he takes with his tape. He sets the figures down in a column, and he could give this set of half a dozen figures to any tailor in the world, I suppose, and the other man would know what each one refers to by its place in the column.

An Eskimo woman who never saw or heard of a tailor employs an almost identical system. Dorila Theroux, one of the best bush pilots in eastern Canada, was describing to me how he ordered a parka and the Eskimo woman took a string. She measured him across the shoulders and tied a knot. Then she measured him around the chest and tied another knot. She took his sleeve length, tied another knot, and so on, until she had a piece of cord twelve feet long containing a series of knots along its length.

"Granted," said Dorila, "a parka does not have to fit like a dress coat. But the parka this woman made for me fitted to perfection, a tailor-made job if ever there was one."

Theroux made one spectacular flight from Great Whale on Hudson Bay to Fort Chimo, and to have a souvenir of that little jaunt across the sub-arctics, he asked the Eskimos to make him a cap of the kind he saw the men wearing.

One of the Eskimo women came and studied Dorila's head for a minute or two. She took no measurement. She just looked and calculated. In one night, that woman crocheted the cap which Dorila now wears, a dark red, round Cossack cap, with Eskimo designs worked into its fabric, and a fine tassel pendant.

The talents of the handicrafters, of course, are with us everywhere; and no matter how mechanized our world becomes, as long as someone remembers for us the old-fashioned way, we are safer than we think.

Slowdown

When a man is young, he never ceases to marvel at the time it takes a woman to dawdle and fiddle and faddle in front of mirrors and in the bathroom, preparing herself for the light of day.

When a man is young, he can slosh himself in the shower in one minute, shave in two, give his hair a swipe with the comb, and leap full-panoplied into life's arena and ready for the fray.

But, as the years go by, a man begins to slow down. He starts taking a little longer over the basin in the morning. Shaving, for example, becomes a bit of a chore. The years bring increasing wrinkles, grooves, hollows, and depressions in his once rounded visage. His whiskers grow coarser. Razors grow duller. His hand appears to be losing some of its courage. Where, in his twenties, he used to sweep his razor over his face, now he whittles, in small careful scrapes.

When a man reaches the age when he has to have false teeth, the time spent over the morning wash basin begins to assume alarming proportions. These useful and comforting articles require about four or five times the number of minutes it took to brush the old personal teeth.

And as for the hair, even a bald man can't save time: he has to wash his pate as thoroughly as he does his cheeks and chin.

Sometime after a man is fifty, he wakens to the fact that instead of three minutes, his toilet takes twelve; and it shocks him to note that where his wife used to take twelve, now she whips through the job in three.

Canoe: The Exacting Servant

An acquaintance who very nearly lost a precious twelve-year-old child by drowning wants a warning published about the vicious, treacherous canoe.

The canoe is not, of course, either vicious or treacherous. With the wheel, the loom, and a few other things, it is one of the most valuable of human inventions. I don't know how Europe or Asia were explored, but it was the canoe that opened up the vast wealth and beauty of America. And the bark canoe, at that. A canoe very like the article you buy in the stores today. We must all admit that it was the French Canadians, equipped with the birch-bark canoe of the northern Indians, in all sizes from fifteen feet to forty feet in length, who first explored the great West and down the Mississippi.

The canoe is beautiful, manageable, portable, a work of art. Nobody should be allowed to enter a canoe until willing and able not merely to paddle it, but to lift it from the water to its resting place on shore, rather than drag it up as if it were a keeled boat. If they are not old enough to understand they must treat it as a fragile thing of beauty, to be cared for, to be lifted, to be guarded from bumping into docks, rocks, snags, boulders, to be coddled and cared for, they are not old enough to be allowed to use it.

The boy of twelve to whom I referred above had no more right to be alone in a canoe than in a sports car going fifty miles an hour.

The Indians who invented the canoe never paddled more than a few yards from shore even on calm days. If an Indian had to get across a lake a mile wide, he would paddle three miles around its shore. The tremendous journeys the Indians and voyageurs made up the St. Lawrence, through the hundreds of miles of the Great Lakes and up through continuations of the Great Lakes far across the northwest, were all made hugging the shore. And they were interrupted for days at a time when the water was too rough along those shores. Champlain's journals and the Jesuit Relations bear this fact out.

To this day, Indians and woodsmen can always spot a greenhorn in the wilds when they see a canoe in the middle of a lake or river.

"Besides," say the Indians, "what is to be seen far out from the shore? Just water. It is close along the shore that everything of interest is to be found. There is more wisdom in one mile of shore than in ten miles of bush or a hundred miles of water."

So, for all the reasons we can think of, a good canoeman is the along-the-shore man.

Discovery

Sometimes you glance at a girl whose beauty makes your heart stand still; but on second glance, all the beauty has vanished.

Then there is the girl you have looked at a thousand times, maybe all your life; and suddenly, to your astonished eyes, she is beautiful, and remains beautiful.

A bachelor friend of mine had gallivanted far into his thirties before the atomic blast of love got him. He was one of those devotees of feminine beauty for whom, ever since his sixteenth year, a new beauty would oust the old one in about thirty days, on the average. I think he had one sweetheart who lasted from May to October, six months; but that was in his mid-twenties, and it was a particularly beautiful summer, filled with full moons and continuously seductive weather. Indeed, most of us felt his hectic search was ended. But it wasn't.

His great weakness was what might be called his second glance. At first glance, he was overwhelmed by the beauty or charm or grace of a new girl. He would rush her furiously. But then, very soon, he would discover on second glance that she was hardly perfect. Soon after that discovery, he would find not two or three, but up to ten or even twenty flaws and imperfections. We thought in time that he was going to be a life-long bachelor. But he wasn't.

His secretary was no breath taking beauty. She was just about the nicest girl you ever met, trim, stylish, more comfortable-looking every year of her thirty years. My Lothario friend had shared his office with her for twelve years.

One day he looked at her over the office desk and burst into tears.

"Good heavens!" he gasped, staring joyously.

They were married last week.

<hr>

Who's Next?

Nearly all of us are agreed that mass production is far ahead of other industrial processes, and that the clothes we wear, the food we eat, the houses we live in, the cars we ride in are far better when produced expertly by the latest triumphant practices of our wonderful century. Yet still there are a few little old carpenter shops and cobbler shops and shirt makers upstairs on side streets of the business section, and repair shops, and people who will paint and refinish old furniture or mend broken chinaware or rebind with ancient leather and gold some precious old book.

An executive acquaintance of mine, a three-car man, attended an auction sale of the effects of one of his late relatives, and to help out, he bought a beautiful old walnut dresser that had come out from England in pioneer times; an antique treasure. He took it to a small cabinetmaker's shop he had noticed downtown.

"I want," he said, "a small hole cut there in the back panel of the dresser to put a clock in. A small electric clock. It will look good ...."

The cabinetmaker instantly refused to do the job, in no uncertain terms.

"But good grief," protested the executive, "it's mine, isn't it? Can't I do what I like with it?"

"It is yours," said the cabinetmaker grimly, "for the time being. But presently, it will belong to somebody else. And I refuse to ruin so beautiful a piece of furniture on the whim of a temporary owner."

That's the stuff to give 'em.

The above report of a cabinetmaker's stand brought a letter from a reader in Alberta:

"During the war, three other officers and I called on the late R.B. Bennett, Lord Bennett he was then, on his lordly estate in the south of England, not far from where we were camped. Lord Bennett showed us graciously over the beautiful big house and gardens and told us its history, what previous nobles had owned the property over the past centuries.

"He then took us to a balcony and showed us in the distance the outer boundaries of his estate, east, north, and west. And when he paused, and we gazed at the domain, a captain in our party asked innocently:

23

"'I wonder who will own it next?'

"Lord Bennett turned a dark turkey crimson and escorted us to the front portico."

⁂

Weather: The Redeeming Spoiler

The uncertainty of the weather becomes more and more important to us as we become more and more organized, regimented, sheltered, perfected. One by one, we are mastering all the forces that surround us, in the earth, the sea, the air. Production in industry is becoming a law itself. Without realizing it, or even understanding it when we do realize it, we are becoming slaves. Through our own perfectionism, we can become a race of healthy, magnificent, perfectly-served, eternally comfortable and secure monsters. We will become supermen. And a superman is a very inferior creature to a man. At least a man has still a vestige of freedom.

But the weather may save us. It will always, let us pray, remind us of greater powers than our own. I find myself, as I grow older, welcoming the surprising day, the disappointing day. I go to bed on a lovely calm evening. About me moves the ordered world, all magnificently under control, vital, swift, obedient to every need, man made, perfect. It basks, it goes softly to sleep under a benign and tender heaven.

But in the night, I am waked by the patter of rain. The thunder mutters. In a matter of minutes, the storm is raging, the streets are flooded, traffic runs and hides, lights go out. By morning, a grey and ragged day of storm is in full rage. Nobody is comfortable, trains and buses are delayed, power is off, business drops away downtown, and in the big factories the calm executives walk masterfully about their large plants, looking uneasily at the time clocks and the cards the so-called employees have and have not struck into the machines that click and ring bells like cash registers.

Brother, those aren't employees. Those are men and women who have been afraid and upset and disorganized by a little thunderstorm, a mild fillip of weather. Like chipmunks, they scuttled into their holes from the rain.

No, sir, the weather may save us yet, by freezing us, frying us, soaking us, and eternally, let us hope, surprising us.

Fish Stories, Attested

Here is a fish story, eminently attested, that I consider one of the greatest. Alex Forbes, the well-known Canadian sportsman, was fishing for salmon some years ago in the Mistassini River in Quebec. The club members drew lots and then fished the consecutive pools thereafter in rotation, day by day. Alex was fishing the best pool of the river, the Dish pool, when he hooked a large twenty-pound salmon, and after a brief fight, the knot holding the nine-foot gut leader separated, and the fish was lost, with fly and nine-foot leader in its jaws.

The following day, Alex was fishing the next pool upstream, called the Platform pool. This was a small, deep cauldron of water, fished from a rock called the Platform. You could not really cast on this pool. All you could do was dunk your fly with a short line, allowing it to swirl around in the deep, rushing, and agitated water that leaped from above into it. Not many fish were caught here, fewer landed. It was a tough spot.

Alex was drawing in his line for a fresh toss when it tightened. Alex reeled up, and found to his astonishment that he was into a fish all right, but his own fly had hooked onto another leader.

The miraculous part of this tale is that Alex's fly had caught not on the leader, but in the very loop, the one-inch loop on the end of the leader he had lost the day before; otherwise it would not have held.

And he fought the twenty-pounder in that narrow and difficult pool, and the guide at last netted it, proving from the fly and leader that it was indeed Alex's.

It is not uncommon, when trolling for lake trout or other deep fish, to hook somebody's lost line that has broken, especially copper wire line. And not infrequently, there is a fish still on, though generally only the lure.

The only miracle I am a witness to occurred when a large muskellunge of twenty-three pounds broke the line of my canoe companion on his first leap. He continued to leap frantically to try to dislodge the large plug stuck to the end of his snout, and leaped right into the canoe. I claimed this muskie, because I was paddling, and had the canoe where it was when the muskie fell into it.

Legalistic points like that are part of the glee of fishing.

A View From Seventy

We are told that the basic needs of man are food, shelter, and that old devil, sex. What comes fourth is a matter of wide conjecture, but after viewing the parade now for seventy years today (September 25, 1962), it is my opinion that self-esteem is the fourth deep need of man. There are those who work at self-esteem day and night, from birth to death. In the more fashionable levels of society, it is called status seeking these days, but even on the humblest levels, there are men who esteem themselves solely on the basis of their strength, and women who cherish their self-esteem on the basis of their cookies or scalloped potatoes.

Most of us base our self-esteem on our virtues. But some esteem themselves on their vices. Confirmed criminals, as any psychologist will tell you, esteem themselves not only on their successful crimes but even on the number of years they have spent in prison. I have known drunks whose self-esteem sprang from the number of times they had been drunk in a month, far drunker than anybody else you could mention.

Self-esteem can be based on prosperity, good looks, physical strength, wit, a talent such as a singing voice, or the ability to play a guitar, figure skate, cook, play chess, checkers, tiddly-winks.

When you have nothing whatever on which to base your self-esteem, neither possessions nor talents nor brains nor comeliness, you can always esteem yourself for your race and creed.

And after looking at those who are loudest in pride of their race and creed over less blessed individuals, I am inclined to believe that they have no other grounds for self-esteem.

When the Beauty Shop Sign was a Shaving Mug

A barber shop, from the moment you settle into the enveloping chair, is one of the pleasantest, drowsiest, most becalming places imaginable. You are tucked in. You gaze modestly, but not without interest, at yourself in the big mirror. The barber gets your instructions. The soothing shears begin. A lovely peace invades you. You drowse. You waken only to add some little trifle of additional advice. You decide to have a facial . . .

And a shampoo.

And you remember, dreamily, that this self-pampering is entirely excusable, having a historic association with a long tradition of male partiality for the soothing ministrations of the beauty parlour.

As recently as when I was a boy, which is sixty years ago, all but one of the beauty parlours in town were for men. There were dozens of them. They were called barber shops, of course, but bore little or no resemblance to the poor little one-horse, hair-cutting barber shops of today.

They were busy from morning to night, and I mean night, which was 10:00 P.M., attending to the facial ornamentation and glamorization of men. Not some men, but nearly all men. It was the days of straight razors, and everybody from hod carriers up to bankers with a dime to spare went to the barber to be shaved, shampooed, massaged with magenta creams, a long, lovely, leisurely progression of steaming towels, head-ducks in marble basins, dreamy wobbles of the scalp, fragrant manipulation of the facial muscles, tonicked, scented and finally powdered. With the tiers of shelves of gilt-inscribed mugs, the nickel-plated massage machines, the mirrors, the male beauty salons of fifty years ago were much more spectacular than the female beauty parlours of today.

The single female beauty parlour of those days was pat-ronized only by the thin top layer of the ultra-fashionable ladies. They were said to have their faces "enamelled," and were unable to smile. But the generality of girls and women, in 1900, had to be beautiful naturally. No faking.

Barnyard Language

When a duck feels a quack coming on, it quacks. There is no rhyme or reason to a duck's quacking. Chickens do not speak unless they have something to say. Occasionally, a hen, with an egg on her mind, will go about mildly squawk-ing in an absent-minded way. After she has laid an egg, she is likely to burst forth in a loud cackle of jubilation. But for the rest of the time, she goes about with few remarks, except to ejaculate briefly over the pleasures of having found a tid-bit on the ground.

A hen is a very thoughtful, reasonable conversationalist. But a duck is plain silly. Without reference to anything that is being said by other ducks, and apropos of nothing that is happening around it, it goes about, its stomach barely clear of the ground, quacking soft, quacking loud, and now and then rearing up with wide eyes to engage in a regular fusil-lade of resounding quacks.

In winter such ducks as have escaped the oven and are alive, are confined to barracks. You will find them in stables and barns, corralled in one of the unused horse stalls. To lean on the rail and observe a group of winter ducks imparts a very comfortable sense of self-respect in you. After all, the public men of the world, who have been quacking away at international meetings for years aren't as bad as ducks. At least they don't drag their stomachs on the ground.

The Toss-up

One of my cronies is a man constitutionally incapable of making up his mind. Indecision is not only natural to him, he seems to delight in it.

His usual course, when faced with a decision, is to toss a coin.

"Heads I do," he says, firmly, "tails I don't."

Up goes the coin and comes down heads.

"Two out of three," he says quickly, tossing the coin.

It comes down heads again.

"Three out of five," he exclaims anxiously.

It comes down heads once more, deciding the matter, as you might say, decisively. It means he does what he was doubtful of, beyond any doubt.

"Did I say heads I don't," he asks, "or heads I do?"

By this time, you realize that the poor fellow has made up his mind backwards. He really didn't want to do whatever it was. But it took all the hocus-pocus of tossing a coin, welching on that, and then defrauding himself at the end, to make him realize his decision.

And I may add when he accepts the decision, it is with the darkest misgivings.

Reconstruction

A new-Canadian friend of mine is an expert carpenter and cabinetmaker who is having a little difficulty with the English language.

His favourite topic is "remuddling." He has built up an excellent trade in "remuddling" some of the older houses in town. Actually, he does an expert and imaginative job. But his best effort, it seems to me, has been introducing a dandy new word into our contemporary vocabulary. For when some of our town planners go to work to remodel old districts, or when our traffic experts proceed to remodel our problem thoroughfares, they succeed only in "remuddling." And certainly a great many of us who have been faced with the job of remodelling our summer cottages, most of which require drastic surgery after a few years, come up with some remarkable muddles.

A newspaper colleague recently bought a summer cottage of about 1920 vintage. He got it at a very reasonable price, figuring to remodel it to present-day standards. The remodelling, he discovered, was going to cost more than he paid for the cottage. So he is going to spend his vacation doing the "remuddling" himself, and it is sure to be a masterpiece.

Campsite Manners

The establishment of public campsites along the highways is now general in all provinces across Canada. The behaviour of the public in these accommodations, most of which are free or require a very small fee, is the subject of considerable concern to the provincial superintendents responsible for these parks.

An Ontario superintendent reports such things as a porcelain sink and its fittings torn from the wall of a comfort station and just left lying on the floor. More than two hundred recently planted trees in one park were pulled out of the ground and left to die in the sun, a total loss. In another site, some wit bolted ninety-six doors from the inside in the change houses for the bathing beach by some means not yet discovered. Apart from such instances of sheer mischief, many of the camps are left in dirty condition, the trash-cans ignored, fireplaces left filthy, bottles and broken glass strewn about.

One superintendent, on the other hand, reported an elderly lady taking her husband, who had a badly damaged heart, on what might be his last camping trip, and leaving her campsite as follows:

She scrubbed the campsite table, removed the garbage and sprayed the container, cleaned out the fireplace, and laid a fresh pile of fuel wood from the wood pile at the outskirts of the site. Gathered a separate heap of kindling. And brought the camp ranger a pie she had left over on departure.

This proves there are at least two kinds of people in the world.

Card Trick

After leaving the ladies downstairs for a social evening with the TV, I went upstairs to my friend's den and found him busy sorting through a great pile of Christmas cards he was about to tie up in a bundle and put away somewhere until next December, when he would get them out to remind him to whom to send next Christmas's cards.

He appeared to be searching for something in particular.

"Ah, here it is!" he cried, picking out the card.

He had an envelope ready, and carefully he inserted this

card with another one already in the envelope, and set them aside. Then he tied up the bundle.

"What's so special about those two?" I asked.

"Well," he said, "a couple of our friends have had a quarrel and they're not speaking to one another. It's been going on since last summer. They've made it rather embarrassing for all of us who know them both.

"So, if they haven't patched it up by next Christmas, I am going to send them these cards that they sent us. I'll keep them nice and fresh . . . ."

"You mean?"

"Sure," he said slyly. "They'll get cards from each other, and each will think the other has relented. And all will be forgiven."

Sneaky.

Culture is Where We're At

When some of our more genteel illuminati, on TV or radio or in the press, deplore the absence of culture in Canada, relics of a fast vanishing era get the willies. Do they not see culture sweeping over us like a rising tide?

Our food is cultured, our fields are cultured, our herds, our hens, our drinking water are cultured. The air we breathe is cultured by air conditioning. The latest news is that our wilderness is being cultured. As fast as we can cut down the rude forest, which grew as it liked, we are planting new trees, chosen trees, cultured trees, not to grow as they like, of course, but in beautiful straight rows.

The genteel folk, of course, suppose they are talking about another form of culture, the cultivation of the mind, the cultivation of the taste – art, music, literature, the dance – and also the art of lofty and enlightened conversation.

But it is, of course, all the same thing. Culture, in its barest and largest sense, means improvement by considered alteration.

And all the massive forces of mankind, as expressed in industry, politics, science and art, are swollen with purpose to improve.

So it is safe to say that within one hundred years, they will not be able to find, in the whole round world, a single living thing that grew the way it wanted to grow; nor any living soul that has not been trimmed to perfection like a show poodle. Culture, not atomic fission, is likely to be the end of man.

———❀———

Veal

It was a small restaurant off the main streets and said to be a haunt of gourmets. There were only a dozen customers present when we dropped in rather late for dinner. From the menu in French I chose veal cutlets done in hunter-style. I like veal, and hunters.

What came was surprising. Veal is naturally tender, if only by reason of its youth. But this veal was cut in thin slices, which had been sauteed or browned before being combined with the sauces and vegetables that made it hunter-style. It was as hard, stringy, and chewy as a ham steak that has been fried too much.

As is the custom in gourmet haunts, the chef came out for a little visit with his guests, and when he came to our table I mentioned that the veal was a little tough and stringy.

"Of course," said the chef. "It is the vehicle for the fine sauces of the dish, as conceived in the recipe. It is deliberately made to be chewy for that reason."

"But I like the taste of veal," I protested.

"Good heavens!" said the chef. "Anybody can cook veal to taste like veal!"

<hr />

The Rustlers

On the one hand, as my Old Man used to say, there is time. And on the other hand, money. The chemical you use to convert time into money is a thing called work.

Up around Sault Sainte Marie, if you have a little time on your hands, you can go to the local forestry office and obtain a permit to go into the crown lands and cut yourself a little pulp wood. It's chemistry, like. Her Majesty is always willing to let you convert a little time into money.

Well, sir, this Thessalon man got his permit, signed all the proper papers, armed himself with all the pamphlets and legalities as to his behaviour in the bush, and was given a precise map location as to where he could cut so many cords of pulpwood: spruce, balsam, and poplar.

After three days' cutting, he had two cords of spruce and balsam, all neat and four feet long, and three cords of poplar. And he piled them neat as a soldier on the bank of a little creek near by. And then he went out for three days' rest.

When he got back, there was the spruce and balsam. But all the poplar was gone, every last stick of it. In the mud, he could see signs which indicated that the creek had been employed as a means of larceny.

Down the creek a quarter of a mile, he found a beaver lodge and his three cords of poplar firmly wedged into the structure for the winter rations.

Beaver don't qualify for permits.

———※———

Who Looks?

In a downpour I ducked into a shop doorway to wait for the deluge to slacken. And a man ducked in right behind me. He was carrying a rolled-up umbrella.

"Why don't you put up your umbrella?" I asked.

"It is all full of holes," he said. "It's all worn along the ribs."

"Then, er . . . um," I questioned naturally.

"To tell the truth," he said, "all my life I have wanted to carry a walking stick. But I haven't got the nerve. I would have the life kicked out of me at the office. But whenever it looks like rain, I get the chance to do the next best thing. I carry this umbrella. I get some of the satisfaction I would get out of a stick."

"I see you are a very honest man," I admitted.

"Well, I see you are carrying a stick," he replied. "That's why I told you. How do you get the nerve to carry a stick?"

"I'll show you," I said. And when the rain slackened, I took his rolled-up umbrella and handed him my stick. And we walked proudly down the two blocks to where our ways parted, where we changed back.

"See?" I said. "Who cares?"

If we only realized how seldom people think of us, we wouldn't worry about what they think of us.

Fiction

There is a pretty snide trick played on one another by those intellectuals who read all the latest books. I had lunch with two of them.

"Say, Harry," said Willmot, "have you read *Surmise of Our Time* yet?"

"I enjoyed it," said Harry, hiding in his coffee cup.

"What did you think," asked Willmot, "of the chapter on the Himalayas? Where Dixon got stuck in that crevasse?"

"Clever," agreed Harry. "I think the suspense was handled better than anything since that scene in *Macabre*, remember, where Lilian had to stand all that time under the crystal chandelier?"

"Ah, yes," said Willmot. "That was sheer agony for the reader, I confess."

They were referring to a couple of recent best sellers.

Harry left before Willmot and me.

"There *is* no chapter about the Himalayas in *Surmise*," gloated Willmot. "And nobody by the name of Dixon! What a phony Harry is!"

Back at the office, Harry phoned me.

"Did you hear me trick Willmot?" he chortled. "There's nobody by the name of Lilian in *Macabre*, and nothing about any chandelier! What a fraud he is!"

They are both happy in their erudition.

———※———

Midnight Onions

On a recent hunting trip, I had a couple of nights in camp with some Americans who were passing through to deeper territory. One of them was a doctor, and a more sinewy, leathery old cuss of close to seventy I never encountered. He had many amusing things to say about health.

"Why do we crave?" he asked. "Why have we been given the capacity to crave, if it weren't of some practical important use? My belief is that when we hanker after something, like pickles, or tomato juice, a salt herring or a feed of fried chicken, it is merely our system calling, as clearly as if it were shouting to us, for certain chemicals those particular foods will supply, and which our system is in need of. I don't think our systems are inarticulate. I honestly believe that they can speak to us, and that they do.

"Among animals, you will see that craving expressed in a sudden desire for some unusual food: a dog eating grass, a cow chewing its stall, a horse eating rope. Often these are signs that the animal is ill, but if so, it may be ill because it isn't getting what its system requires either to keep it healthy or to combat the illness.

"This seems to me to be true of us humans too. Maybe we get a craving for something that is really bad for us, like sugar for a diabetic. In that case, the craving is a signal from our system that things are out of kilter, and need to be looked into. But nine times out of ten, a sudden craving for a particular item of food, whether it is a routine food like beef or some unusual delicacy like anchovies, is merely a call from some particular portion of our system for an urgently needed ingredient of its particular process or function. For example, right now have you gentlemen got any onions in camp?"

We all rose from our bunks and stools and accompanied the old rascal, though it was a way past 10:00 P.M. and our bed time, as honest hunters, to the camp kitchen where we found a bag of big, rough, hot onions. And with camp bread, we each made a whopping big sandwich of thick-sliced onions, seasoned with salt and pepper, with a dollop of mayonnaise, a squirt of Worcestershire sauce, a dribble of vinegar, a dash of mustard, and a sprinkle of anything else that was handy. And we all went to bed healthy.

———❁———

Blanked Out

"Where," asked the elderly lady ahead of me in the bus line, "do I get the bus for Forest Hill?"

"This is it," replied the bus driver. "All you got to do, lady, is look up overhead there, at the sign."

The lady got in and I sat across from her.

"There's too many signs," she puffed. "I gave up looking at them long ago."

She is right. This is the age of inattention. Our attention is demanded beyond its capacity. Long before we step out the front doors of our homes, we have had to pay attention to a score of things: things that demand attention, such as the buttons and switches that turn off the light, the electric stove, the toaster, the electric blanket, the radio. A few years ago, only a few years, we did not even have to remember to lock our back and front doors when we went out. We fixed the damper on the kitchen stove, when breakfast was over. Then peace descended.

When we do step out the front door, our attention is instantly demanded by traffic. We have to be alert for our lives. And if we let our attention wander, for an instant, we are likely to be swiped. The minute we are outside, everything clamours for our attention. People dress to be noticed. By the time we reach the shops, we are caught up in a violent hurricane of advertising, merchandise display, and public relations. Garish signs blink, red, blue, and gold. Traffic signals, like fleas, jump from green to yellow to red. Cars shout their horns for our attention, bus exhausts blat. Out over the transoms of shops, loudspeakers blast music and song. Newsboys rant, cops blow shrill whistles, sirens howl, holy people on street corners shove leaflets at us, nut houses waft the odour of frying cashews out their doors, a legless man on the edge of the pavement waves his yellow pencils up at us . . .

And is our attention drawn? I doubt it. The holes in our heads through which we are supposed to receive impressions of the world around us grow smaller and more calloused around the edges with each passing year. There is only one refuge for us: inattention.

The Vaccination

As far as I can recall, it is years and years since anybody has grasped me by the upper left arm. Or even the upper right arm. My friends usually seize me by the hand, the elbow or occasionally by the forearm. To greet me, to restrain me, to emphasize a point, they will make a grab at some part of my brachial limbs. But never, as nearly as I can now painfully recollect, do they grab my upper arm, especially my upper left arm.

But I have been vaccinated, for an impending trip to London to look at the Queen.

It was within the last three weeks the operation was performed. A nasty blister rose on my arm. It itched. It was sore. It sent shadowy pangs of pain down my arm, up my shoulder, out to my fingers.

And almost everybody I know in the world has, within the past three weeks, grabbed me by the upper left arm, whopped me enthusiastically on the upper left arm, gripped me and swung me around to meet their joyous friendly gaze, sneaked up behind me in crowded department stores to enclose my upper left arm in a vice-like grip for no reason whatever but to whirl me around and say hello.

Throughout an adventurous and not entirely blameless life, I have been curiously free of interference by the police. I have seen my friends and boon companions picked up by the nape of the neck by the police, I have seen them given the heave-ho by the constabulary and *gendarmerie* of sundry lands. Yet not until two days ago has a cop ever laid hands on me. I was rather proud of this distinction. But day before yesterday as I was about to step off the curb at an intersection, a policeman seized my arm to save me from being clipped by a car. And where do you suppose he seized me?

You're right. When I got home, I told my dear wife about my misfortunes of the day.

She patted me affectionately on the blister.

Winter Bounty

On a recent trip into the north, I visited some Indian friends whom I knew as guides during the fishing season and who are now on their winter trapline. They were living in what we would consider squalor until we recollect how our Canadian pioneer ancestors lived, in their log cabins and shanties in the early days of settlement a hundred and more years ago. Indeed, I have often seen equal apparent squalor in the homes of present-day settlers on our frontiers. It is not squalor, but the natural gypsy extemporization of those dwelling in what they know, or hope, to be temporary quarters.

It was an extremely cold day on which I visited them, and their shelters were pretty flimsy. They had erected rough log enclosures, about four to five feet high, and these were roofed by tents. The tents were erected, in short, upon the low log foundations. Inside, they had camp stoves, and their beds were the conventional balsam-bough mattresses on which their blankets were laid. There was little room, of course, to turn around.

My most familiar friend detected my distress when I joined him in his home.

"You think," he said, "the winter is tough for the Indians. It is our best and happiest season. We never eat better. In the snow, every animal leaves his tracks. We do not have to travel very far before we know how many rabbits, partridge, deer, moose are in the area. It is no trick to find them and trap or shoot them.

"Besides, all we catch keeps, which can't be said of the other season of the year. In winter, we always have food hung up. Of course, our trapping is done in winter, which is our main income, and is possible because of the snow and the frozen lakes and ponds. About all you can say for summer is that it is warm.

I doubt if my Indian friend was pulling my leg. His wife and family looked well-fed and healthy and full of quiet laughter. Meat was hanging on the trees outside. I could see canned goods stashed under boxes and shelves. Reversed beaver skins were stretched on their stretchers, as well as numbers of smaller skins including even squirrels.

"Winter," he said, "is our big time."

What's New

When we travel in a jumbo aircraft, whistling through the sky, we cannot help but think of the vast difference between it and the planes we remember in earlier days. What we ought to do, of course, is reflect on their sameness. The remarkable thing about them both is their sameness in the most important thing of all. They both fly. The old orange crates of the twenties, and the jet screechers share the basic, the all-important feature: they fly.

Probably the silliest thing about us, in the eyes of the twenty-first century, will be our enormous self-satisfaction. The improvements we have made! What a marvellous generation we have been.

But we still eat loaves of bread, as the Babylonians did, as the Romans did a couple of centuries before Christ, while they too were stupefying the world with their wonders of civilization. We still live in square houses, on streets, and the very latest designs of architecture bear more and more resemblance to the houses they had in Ur of the Chaldees. We still wear cowhide on our feet, and wool and cotton or linen (or a feeble substitute thereof) on our bodies. We still wash the dishes in a dishpan, as they did in their kitchens in Egypt a couple of thousand years the other side of A.D. We still get up in the morning, eat breakfast, work, have lunch, work, eat dinner, sit around, go to bed in a square bed, as they did ten thousand years ago, we still gather in crowds to be amused. But the most amusing thing is the sameness of the amusements of Sophocles' time and ours. We still like to get about and see the world, as the pilgrims did when they went on foot or by camel or by ship with three tiers of oars.

Corrected

There has been for many years a prominent mercantile family in Canada by the name of Michie. And everybody pronounces it Mickey.

In North Africa, I met a gentleman of the Fifty-first Highland Division who informed me his name was Mee-hee. On my enquiring how he spelled it, he said Michie.

"That's Mickey," I enlightened him.

"Mee-hee," he asserted, with that curious assurance of the Scots.

"Man," I protested, with all the dignity of an Ontarian, "everybody knows it's Mickey."

But we got on very well despite the man's ignorance. Not one month later, in Italy, I encountered another Scot, and when I asked him his name, he said it was Mitchie.

"How do you spell it?" I enquired suspiciously.

"Michie," said he.

"That's not Mitchie," I snorted. "It's Mickey."

"In the part I come from," said the Scot, quite belligerently, "it is pronounced Mitchie."

And since he was obviously determined to have it his own way I let him go on in his error.

It is a very complex world we live in. Each of us is sure of his own ground. Just because we happen to be born with a name, we assume we know how to pronounce it. Just because we happen to have a certain capacity for knowledge or the opportunity to acquire it, we assume we have all knowledge. Then, of course, there are the characters among us who like to tell other people how to pronounce their own names.

These last are a great help in the world. And the world is full of them.

Telephone Trouble

One of my more lawless friends has had a telephone hangup lately with a neighbour, a lady with a richly cultivated voice, who persists in dialling my friend's number in mistake for her grocer's.

There is only one digit difference in the two telephone numbers. But despite the fact that she has made the mistake a score of times in a few weeks, she never seems to learn. In her grand duchess manner, the moment my friend says hello, she begins:

"Send me right away two dozen eggs, a pound of buttah, five pounds of whate sugah ..."

Formerly, my lawless friend, in a lawless voice, would rudely bawl: "Aw, you've got the wrong number!" And hang up.

But lately, he has thought of a better idea. As soon as Mrs. Topdraw begins her haughty order over the phone, my friend promptly says, "Yes, ma'am, yes ma'am," as though he were taking the order down diligently. When she has finished, he assures her the order will be delivered immediately. Then he goes out into the garden and feels good.

Three times in a week he was enabled to pull this prank on Mrs. Topdraw. It was amusing to sit in the garden and imagine Mrs. Topdraw indignantly telephoning the grocer and demanding to know why the order had not come. But then my friend's conscience begins to trouble him on the grocer's behalf. Perhaps his little joke might be costing the innocent grocer a lot of trouble as well as the loss of a good customer. So, he dropped into the grocery store and explained his trouble and outlined his little prank, in all candour, to the grocer.

"That woman!" exploded the grocer hotly. "I've tried every way I know to get rid of her. She's more nuisance than all the rest of my customers put together!"

Which gives rise to the reflection: maybe those who are a nuisance to anybody are a nuisance to everybody.

Cities

A taxi driver in Montreal, presuming I came from Toronto, asked me which city I preferred. To disconcert him, I told him I came from Winnipeg, but spent a great deal of my time in Victoria.

"Which city do you prefer?" he pursued doggedly.

"Halifax," I told him. "I love seafood."

"You can get wonderful seafood right here in Montreal," corrected the taxi driver.

"It's imported," I parried. "In Halifax, it grows."

"I never been in Halifax," admitted the taxi driver, "but Montreal has got everything. I been in New York at that."

"Good seafood in New York," I agreed. "Also in Bari."

"Ontario?" checked the taxi driver.

"No, Italy," I evaded. "Wonderful seafood."

Coming to a stop light, the taxi slowed, and the driver turned around and had a good look at me.

"Seafood," he said. "Haven't you got a favourite city?"

And for the first time in my life, the idea occurred to me that it is as wicked to have a favourite city as it is to have a favourite among your children; or to prefer your father to your mother. If you back up far enough away from the subject, you perceive that a city is not an institution, but a personality. Any one of them can be, may be, some day your home. In any one of them may be that "stranger, across a crowded room," whose laughter will sing in your dreams. In each of them are streets, vistas, spires, angles of misty beauty, bookstores, race tracks, philatelic clubs or whatever in the world your love and hobby is. And people, fabulous people, as lonely and searching and single as you, swarming the wintry streets, peering, wondering . . .

"Montreal," asserted the taxi driver, as the light changed, "has got everything."

Derailed

The street car conductor was in an ugly mood. He preferred not to look at his passengers as they filed past him. If obliged to do so, he gave them a sullen glance.

He slammed the door. He slapped tickets and change down on his tiny counter. When he called the name of the stops, it was in a grudging tone half under his breath.

The man was in a bad way. And everybody in the car – other than those happy characters who somehow manage to keep themselves wrapped in a cellophane of unawareness of the world around them – was in some degree conscious of the conductor's mood.

It affected us all in one way or another. Some of us glanced indignantly at him, as though he was a disturber of the peace on this fine spring day. Others, glancing shyly at their neighbours, smiled wryly. I found myself speculating on what it could be that would put a street car conductor into such a sulk. Had he trouble at home? Was his wife ill, or had his daughter run away? No; a man in such plight may look pensive and sad, but not sullen. Had he been hauled out of bed to take an extra tour of duty because some of the younger street railway men were using the flimsy excuse of the cold epidemic to lay off? No; in such case, a man may be in a temper, but it is a glinting and defiant temper which he likes to share with his neighbours. In a case like that, a man likes to talk about it.

Could it be that he had experienced some superb form of discourtesy, to which street car conductors are regularly subjected by saucy citizens? No; it was a deeper, more unreasonable woe than any of these. The conductor had that feeling a woman often has when she just suddenly sits down and has a good cry. I thought to myself what a pity a man can't just go and have a nice sob once in a while.

I took a chance. When I got off, I passed him. And poising

to jump if necessary, I said quietly to him:

"Why don't you just have a good cry?"

He looked at me in astonishment. And his eyes instantly filled with tears.

Tea

There are about a quarter-million Canadians who should hate tea with an abiding passion. In the army, you received a small tin, about the size of a sardine tin, labelled tea. When you opened it, a horrible yellowish powder was disclosed. It was tea, powdered milk, and sugar already mixed and ready to be dumped into a can of hot water and stirred. It was, in the opinion of all true tea drinkers, the nearest we came to defeat in the whole war. It was the most horrible concoction ever invented in the name of austerity and economy.

Tea has a lot of enemies. In the average restaurant, they have a large urn of hot water with a tap under it. The waitress stuffs a tea bag in a pot and runs some of this stale hot water onto it.

In the United States, a waiter brings you a cup and saucer, with a tea bag resting in the cup, and a teapot of water which was probably hot when he started from the kitchen. You are supposed to pour the hot water onto the tea bag in the cup; or, possibly, you immerse the bag in the pot of tepid water. No wonder the Americans are coffee drinkers.

In Galashiels, Scotland, I was buying a book in a little shop and got invited in back to the kitchen for a cup of tea. The teapot was simmering on the back of the stove. They poured for me what looked like and tasted like sepia ink. It was six days before my sense of taste was restored; freckles I had lost in boyhood returned to my cheeks; my grey hair turned red. I am always glad to escape from the Old Country and get back to Canada for a good cup of tea.

This is the way to make it, and it came into my family from Scotsburn, N.S. You put fresh water in the kettle and the minute it starts to boil hard, you take the largest cup in the pantry and put a pinch of tea – with your fingertips – into the cup. Without removing the kettle from the fire, so that the water tumbles boiling out of the spout, you plunge it onto the tea in the cup.

Milk? Never! Sugar? Well, a wee dab on the tip of the spoon if you like. By the time it is cool enough to drink, it is ambrosia.

Uptown Art

The owner of one of those small china and fancy goods shops you find all over the uptown shopping streets was ruddy with anger when she turned to wait on us.

The woman she had been attending walked languidly out the door.

"That fool woman!" fumed the china store lady. "Could she make a spoon, if I gave her all the silver in India?"

"Mmmm," I temporized.

"Could she make a cup?" demanded the saleslady furiously. "If I gave her the finest clay, if I gave her the material for bone china?"

"Umpha," I doubted.

"The haughty..." the saleslady attempted to find the right noun, and then decided it would hardly be polite, and me a stranger.

She stared at me steadily a moment, until her blood pressure subsided.

"Those people," she said, shakily, "give me the pip. They come in here and sneer at all my china, my cups and saucers, my plates, my little mantel ornaments and decorative bits. They say they are tawdry, second-rate, cheap. I admit they aren't up to what you will find in the big expensive downtown shops. But ..."

She swept her little shop with a loving glance.

"Could you," she demanded, "make a single thing you see in this place?"

The lady is quite right. Second-rate art is so far ahead of the tenth-rate talents of the vast majority of us that it deserves a little reflection. If we were stuck with the job of making ourselves a cup, a plate, a spoon, what an absurdity it would turn out to be.

Hail to the big artists of this world, of course. But to all the little artists, hi!

Blawther

The Scottish race is reputed for its dour and taciturn nature. If any people may be said to weight their words, it is the Scotch. But when it comes to blatherskites, Scottish blatherskites may be said to top them all.

You know the kind: the amiable, loquacious, elaborative, fine-spinning, hair-splitting, tenacious, and uninterruptable Caledonian compendium.

An Irish blatherskite is purely lyric. You can easily shut him off. He takes offence easily, and can be sent into the sulks with a mere word.

The English blatherskite is not so lightly handled. He is commonly of two types: the heavy blatherskite who booms in a large and deliberate tone like a retired colonel; or else the light and witty type, a sort of Wodehouse character, who imagines he is killing you. He bubbles, quips, and fizzes. Either kind is generally rude, themselves, and takes no offence when you grow rude and simply crowd them out of the conversation. They wander off to find less valiant victims.

But the Scotch blatherskite is a desperate character. Once he pins you, he pins you not only with his tongue, but with his gimlet eye and his argument. He encourages you to enter the lists of argument, and nails you to your own barn door before you have got half a sentence uttered. Yet this device involves you. You hate to be nailed. He's got you.

The very accent of the Scot, though devised by a race given to few words, lends itself miraculously to the blatherskite. The Irish accent has humour and pathos in it. The English, in all its dialects, has a slightly authoritarian irritant in it. But the Scotch has bullets in it, arrows, javelins, stones, projectiles. When a Scottish blatherskite nails you to your own barn door, he lays such a barrage down around you that you dare not move.

Of course, there are very few Scottish blatherskites.

The Age of Pallor

To be sunburned was a very serious matter, in those days still attached to us by these elderly ladies now romping amongst us in bikinis. Sunstroke lay in wait for a damsel crazy enough to let the summer sun touch her. And as for being suntanned! Brown? Ladies were milk white.

Indeed, they were a sickly white. In 1900, which is only yesterday to some of us, rouge was the mark of the fallen woman. Lipstick belonged to the stage, and to chorus girls walking along the street from the theatre to the hotel, after the show. Ah, what a morbid thrill to pass a bevy of them on the street. Vice, carnality, turpitude, depravity, lipstick, rouge.

With no sun touching their pallor, with no cosmetics sullying their pure waxiness, the females of 1900 looked like something that lived under a log. I realize that there were songs and ballads of the 1800s celebrating the lovely roses that bloomed on the cheeks of the girls, and the ruby lips. The city girls gloried in their achromatism, their etiolation. They looked anaemic. Possibly they were anaemic. I have some old class pictures of my schooldays. The boys looked like contemporary boys. The girls looked like suet. They all wore wide-brimmed hats to keep the sun off them. They hid from the sun. A summer resort, in 1900, was a large hotel with verandahs, awnings. It was not from modesty alone the ladies wore bathing suits from their ears to their ankles. It was for fear of the sun.

Now, if you can't get enough sun, you can buy cosmetics to turn you brown.

Spurious Itch

The lady who waits on me at the library and helps me find the population of Afghanistan in 1600 A.D., and that sort of thing, is a great believer in signs and tokens, superstitions and extrasensory perception. On her holidays, she goes by bus all the way down to Duke University, even in summer when hardly anybody is around there, to revel in the records, statistics, and particulars with regard to second sight, clairvoyance, telepathy, hypnology, thaumaturgy, and hocus-pocus.

But of course she will also not walk under ladders and will back up and go around a block rather than cross a black cat's path.

Three or four days ago, she was excited.

"I'm coming into money," she informed me. "Both my palms are as itchy as anything."

She scratched them enthusiastically in turn.

"Both," she said. "Both palms. That is a sure sign."

"It might be a little eczema," I suggested.

"Nonsense. You can't get eczema on your palms. Anyway, if you are sensitive to psychic forces, you can always distinguish between psychic intimations and ordinary, everyday physical symptoms. Mmmmmm! This is like electricity in my hands. It's been going on for two days now."

She rubbed her palms ecstatically on the tweed hips of her skirt.

Today, when I returned a book, my itchy friend immediately began chattering about the weather and the United Nations, so I knew she was trying to distract me away from the itch.

"Any money yet?" I enquired.

"Do you know what it is?" she said, very crestfallen. "It was an allergy, a reaction to these new benzedrine pills the doctor gave me. All I can say is if modern science is going to disrupt everything like that, how are we going to solve the mysteries of the hereafter?"

"Or the heretobefore," I consoled.

The Pickle

One of my friends who owns a magnificent and intelligent fox-hound allows the dog in the house only at the conclusion of a hunting day. It is a special honour reserved for those occasions. The rest of the time, winter and summer, the hound lives in a fine kennel at the end of the garden.

Not only is he allowed in the house, but he is permitted to sit on the dining-room floor beside his master, while the master feasts. And what is more, from time to time, his lord casts him a tidbit from his own plate. I may never get as near to heaven as this hound comes, sitting there, proud, begging, self-conscious of his glory!

After a wonderful day spent on three foxes over the first fine snow of December, we were dining off cold rare roast beef, baked potatoes with French dressing, and similar hunters' fare. The hound was getting his share. The master winked at me and reached to a dish which contained several large whole dill pickles. Selecting the largest and the juiciest, the master turned and tossed it to the hound.

The poor fellow, seeing this large gift hurtling through the air, caught it with a powerful chop of his jaws. A stunned expression suffused his eyes as he held the sour-salty monstrosity in his molars. He took an experimental chew. Then, very delicately, he bowed his head and laid the dill pickle on the floor.

My friend howled with laughter.

"That," I submitted, "is a heck of a poor joke!"

"Haw, haw, haw!" bellowed my friend, reaching out to rough-handle the head of his hound.

"A dog doesn't like to be laughed at," I quoted.

"Doesn't he?" snorted the lord and master. "Look, men of our stamp, hunting men, are playing jokes on each other all the time. In what way is this dog inferior to my other friends, that I shouldn't play jokes on him ... eh?"

The hound, doggone it, seemed to agree.

Camouflage

Few of us use our normal voices in speaking on the telephone. We nearly all put on some kind of airs. Usually those airs take the form of what we might call high society voice. One minute we are snarling and growling away in our familiar tones and accents. Then the telephone rings, and the instant we pick up the receiver, our whole nature undergoes a miraculous change.

"Hail-o!" we enunciate, in a voice that would make syrup seem sour.

As a matter of fact, the telephone might be employed as a test of character. It has been my observation over a great many years of newspaper reporting that the men and women who have no change of manner, voice, or tone when answering or speaking on the telephone have been, with no exception I can think of, the best, the most reputable, the most distinguished of people. What I mean is this: in interviewing a man or woman, we are talking along, and the telephone rings. Many of those we have to interview in the newspaper business are phonies, stuffed shirts, tambourines, or publicity hounds. These are the ones who, before our very eyes, pick up the receiver and in a twinkling, are transfigured from the person we were talking to one instant ago into another person entirely. Most of these chameleons of character adopt the sweet style. A few affect the reverse as their normal telephone manner: a short, gruff, masterful style.

But the solid characters, the top-drawer people, on picking up the phone, make not the slightest alteration in their voices or manner, speaking into the instrument as simply and unaffectedly as they had been speaking to us the moment before. It has been my experience that these are the people to be trusted.

Even in the home, it is fun to listen to the various airs and attitudes adopted by the members of the family on the phone. You can almost guess who they are talking to by their voices.

What suggested to me that I write this was that an hour ago my wife said:

"Who on earth was that you were talking to on the phone?"

"That was the president of a large corporation."

"You sounded like a deacon," protested my wife.

South'n Frahed and Saccharine

My little sister has been dieting for twenty years. She is middle-aged, but of course does not know it. Middle-aged people are those ten years older than she. She is a nice, plump, chunky little woman who is the right size for her age plus good eating not only for her own sake but as an example to her children. If the cook shies away from her own cooking, what do you expect her children to do? Part of her weight, you might say, is exemplary.

But she is an ardent and, I believe, a typical dieter. She has faithfully tried fourteen diets in the past twenty years. Some of them lasted as long as twenty days. Beyond making her a little dark around the eyes and giving her double chin a curious and unbecoming looseness, I cannot say any of the diets made any change in her.

I had the pleasure of dining with her in Nashville, Tennessee, lately. Nashville is on the highway leading straight up from the Gulf of Mexico, where the shrimp boats are a-comin' all the time. And great big lovely jumbo shrimps are as fresh in Nashville, almost, as they are in New Orleans. Besides, Nashville is in the deep heart of the south'n frahed chicken country. Personally, I have no use for south'n frahed chicken. It seems gluey to me. I don't like to see a chicken cut off practically in its early adolescence. I like a chicken to live on to a ripe old six-pounds weight, and then be roasted, with dressing.

But here in Nashville, my little sister, already speaking with a southern accent, ordered a jumbo shrimp salad to open with. The shrimps were as big as your thumb and forefinger curved before you. Hard, pink, glorious. I think there were eight of them in the salad, together with rich Roquefort dressing. Then came the south'n frahed chicken. My little sister fought with every joint, battled with every muscle and ligament. There were French fried potatoes, rich buttered corn bread, and sundry other fixins. She finished off with a mere dab of Liederkranz cheese and coffee.

When the coffee came, my little sister leaped into action.

"My saccharine!" she cried, reaching for her handbag. "I must have saccharine in my coffee. I'm dieting, you know."

———— ❖ ————

Back Home in Algiers

People are always saying it's a small world. But it isn't. It is a big world. And there are thousands upon countless thousands of us who wander the vast loneliness of the planet and never see a friend. If you look, you can see these lonely ones as you pass in the streets, or sitting in a bus, or at lunch in a restaurant.

It is only a small world when suddenly you find a friend. Then the boundless earth seems suddenly to contract to a little place, with you in the middle of it.

No matter how experienced you may be at being alone in some far end of the world, and no matter how brave or tough you may be, there is always a queer sense of weakness in your bones when you find yourself in a land where you don't know a living soul. One day in the late war, when I was supposed to be in Italy, circumstances took me to Algiers. And in that perfectly unfamiliar looking city, populated with nothing but absolute strangers, I was walking in the crowded street when I saw my brother ahead of me.

My brother was supposed to be in Ottawa. But here he was in Algiers, walking jauntily along like a man heading for his office.

I hastened my steps and fell in beside him.

"What's the name of this street, chum?" I enquired anxiously.

As we had not seen each other for many months, and as both of us believed impossible distance divided us, it was quite a meeting. In less than ten minutes, Algiers was not a strange city at all. The fact that it was full of Arabs and Frenchmen did not seem at all amiss. So suddenly did the earth contract that Algiers seemed to be merely a suburb of the city in which we lived, thousands of miles away. And so it remains in our memory to this day: a familiar community, no distance at all from home.

The Explanation

In a restaurant I frequent, there are five waitresses, four of whom are attractive, pretty girls busy as bees and brimming with good nature. The fifth is sort of a youngish battle-axe. Usually battle-axes are in their fifties and up. But this one is in her mid-thirties. In appearance, she bears no resemblance to her smart young competitors. She doesn't seem to care what she looks like.

And she is crabby. She is crabby with us customers as well as with her sister waitresses. Whenever the proprietor is away from the cash register, she is the one who takes over the post.

Several times, I have been on the point of kidding the proprietor about this lapse in his otherwise good taste. Why would he employ an irascible woman like that, who is in such contrast to the other girls?

It is well I didn't.

She is his wife.

Man's Monstrous Voice

The human voice appears to be the most terrifying sound in nature. Not the howl of the wolf, not the screech of cougar or lynx, not the baleful hoot of the great owl, but the ordinary talking voice of human beings is the sound that petrifies all our fellow creatures in their wild natural state, from warblers no bigger than your thumb up to the deer, moose, grizzly, and the proud moon-raking wolf itself. When the wolf howls and the great horned owl intones its deep five notes, all the wilderness is supposed to freeze in terror. But a couple of children prattling in a passing canoe will send the wolf into the next township, and the owl will depart to some distant hill.

Alex Forbes, a Canadian sportsman with a sensitive understanding of the wilds, showed me this very dramatically. As we passed along a lake in an outboard skiff, we detected three deer on an open hillside of the lakeshore. They stood quietly, watching us approach. Alex signalled for silence, and we passed within seventy-five yards of the deer, who paused in their browsing, eyeing us with a detached sort of interest until we had gone by. They then resumed their quiet feeding. Alex turned the boat and returned along the shore, the same distance out. The deer again raised their heads and studied us calmly, without any appearance of alarm.

Then Alex spoke, in a quiet, normal speaking voice. It was as if we had shot at them; the three deer, electrified, sprang into action and vanished in frantic bounds over the crest of the hill.

Bird-watchers know well that when walking in field or woodlot, if you remain voiceless, your passage is noted without excitement by all the small birds. They come up into the brush tops to observe you. But if you are with a companion, and you talk, the birds seem suddenly to vanish. Chatting however quietly, you can explore a woodlot and never see a single bird, unless some frightened and unidentified hustler in the tree tops. But even if you flounder rather noisily through the brush and tangle, but keep your voice still, you will have the chance to see all the normal occupants of the woodlot.

We read wonderful stories of the mighty grizzly and Alaska brown bear standing up fiercely to the hunters armed with modern magnum rifles. But a guide assured me that one "hello" will send most bears scooting for the next valley at full speed.

We humans have quite a reputation.

The Purists

Oysters being now (in October) in full and fragrant season, it might be the moment to mention some of the evils that surround this ancient and delectable dish. The greatest and most familiar evil is that collection of hot sauces, tomato relish, horse radish and pepper sauce, which is invariably served in the middle of the platter of glorious oysters on the half shell. Louis Jaques and I had the pleasure of the company of Louis's ten-year-old daughter, Penni, at a fine seafood restaurant, and when the oysters arrived, Penni looked at the pretty collection of condiments in the middle and asked:

"What's all that?"

"That," said her father, "is what you put on oysters if you don't like them."

He then explained that there are a lot of people in the world who don't like oysters at all. But such has been the lyric splendour of oyster-lovers, from ancient Roman times right up to the present, that a great many people eat them merely to be fashionable, or to appear cultivated and in the know. In order to get them down, they must paralyze their palates and swallowing muscles with violent and semi-anaesthetic knockout drops of sauce.

"Wouldn't you go," I asked Louis, "for just a little wee squeak of lemon juice?"

Louis looked at me in horror, and then drank one of his oysters off the shell, splinters and all. So I quietly dropped the quarter of lemon I had in my hand, and poked it out of sight.

I have eaten oysters in sundry savoury holes in the wall in Britain, Holland, Spain, Italy, and Germany. My gullet has known the ecstasy of the tiny little inky ones they give you in Marseilles all the way up to the Mattatucks, big as size-eight felt insoles you can get at Billy the Oysterman's in downtown New York. They are all good. But when Jaques is not along, I quietly, discreetly, and after glancing about to see if any gourmet is watching, just put a teeny little wee *pfft* of lemon juice on them. It is evil, but very slightly so.

Stotenbottle

We are unanimous in our detestation of the slowpoke motorist. If anybody makes us sick, it is the driver who dawdles and fiddles and jolts and jerks along in traffic. Our blood pressure rises to 200 when we find the smooth flow of traffic balled up by some old stotenbottle of a motorist who wants to go ten miles an hour slower than the rest of us, who wobbles at intersections, who creeps to stop lights and then takes all of three or even five seconds to get cracking when the lights change.

But when you come to think of it, where would we be without the stotenbottles in traffic? Where would the gaps be in traffic, through which we can pop across, if it were not for the good old stotenbottles who have created a lag? If all drivers were as expert, skilled, smooth, alert as we, traffic would be impenetrable as a rushing river.

The stotenbottles do more than lag. They create marvellous ball-ups at big intersections which cause good three- and four-minute gaps in traffic, thus leaving huge expanses of open road ahead of us in which the smartest of us may exercise our talents, our alertness, our skill in cutting in and beating one another for a good several blocks.

In short, if there were no stotenbottles among us drivers, if we were all as good as we think we are, all expert, all smooth, skilled, alert, we would have no basis for comparison by which we could arrive at the high opinion of ourselves we hold. Next time you encounter a stotenbottle in traffic, instead of allowing your blood pressure to rise, just reflect that he has his uses.

(Note: stotenbottle. This is my grandma's pronunciation of "Stoughton-bottle," which you will find in the larger dictionaries, referring to a large bottle that was used, in the old days, to contain Stoughton's elixir, a fat clumsy, unhandy sort of bottle, always in the way, always getting knocked over. I am a stotenbottle. G.C.)

Domestic Despot in the Dark

With two badly blackened eyes, a colleague arrived at the office with the story that he had bumped into the edge of the door in the dark.

This chap is one of those efficient souls, a disciplinarian. Any business is fortunate to have one of his type on its staff. He is a living reproach to all his subordinates and a comfort to his superiors. It was good to see him with a couple of shiners.

"I have drilled," he grated, to his admiring fellow-workers, "I have drilled it into my family for years never, never leave the bathroom door ajar at night. Everyone of them knows the danger. I have made it an absolute rule. And last night, what do I do? I walk slam into this door!"

It would be hard to know which distressed him the more: the two black eyes, or the failure of his family to obey his laws.

A man who attempts to impose discipline upon so lowly a social organism as the family is definitely looking for two black eyes. Any man who will walk about in his house in the dark, with the confident expectation that all doors are closed and no toys or roller skates are left on the floor is entitled to whatever befalls him. Let us attempt, by all means, to instil a little discipline into the world around us. But at the same time, always walk gingerly in the dark, and keep your hands waving delicately ahead of you. Faith has its place, but not in the dark.

What Was Said?

I had the privilege of almost three hours' conversation with a man in public life who is renowned for his witty discourse. When I got home, all glowing and chuckly, I attempted to impart the highlights of the encounter to my wife.

And I will be jiggered if I could recollect a single remark, a solitary *bon mot*, a joke, or an aside that the great man had uttered. My wife, impatient as I, still delighted and full of reminiscent snickers, fanned the air in the vain attempt to bring to mind anything the bright fellow had said. The harder I tried, the more mildly thunderstruck I became. For the fact was, after a little cool reflection, the famous character had not said anything that was particularly witty, or trenchant or even funny. In the detachment that was possible when out of his hypnotic presence, the fact emerged that the trick of this man's personality is that he adopts a witty air. His eyes glint and sparkle. He opens them and half-closes them as he utters his remarks. His voice has a significant and humorous timbre. While eyeing you with a sly and meaningful expression, he allows his voice to slide and slur in a fashion associated with wit. He leaves sentences half finished, using his hand to gesture airily. Every commonplace, every cliché and platitude is spoken with this arch air of waggery. Most of us have two or maybe three kinds of smiles. This man has fifty.

He is one of the most entertaining of men. He is like those movies and TV programs in which you are amused or convulsed by a comedian, and not one line of which you could recollect ten minutes after the show. In business or politics, such men have to get you on the dotted line, for if you took the goods home and looked them over, the deal would be off.

Shrunk

One of the sadly comic spectacles of this life is the former Lothario, the ex-bon vivant, shuffling and tottering into his old age. Among my fellow students half a century ago was one who was acknowledged to be the Don Juan not only of the college but of the city. A handsome, swashbuckling young man, he trailed a cloud of girls behind him like a charioteer's cloak. And rumour had it that he was to be seen from time to time dining with actresses. This was before the era in which we are liable to have actresses, or at least radio and TV artists, in our own families, and to dine with an actress was turpitude, sheer turpitude.

I forget now; but it could be we envied him, we more freckled and knob-kneed scholars. In the years following our college days I used to see him from time to time, still glamorous, amorous, happy, and festive.

In a department store yesterday I spotted him goutily stumping along amid the shoppers. He had shrunk. His long legs seemed to have hinges in them, and one could almost hear them creak as he lifted them up and set them down. He was trimly dressed in tweed and his hat was rakish, but his neck was now a little too small for his collar. I took his arm and said hello.

"Why, Clark!" he cried gaily. "How you've shrunk!"

Broiled Bones

Many years ago, midway between two wars, I was in London, and a friend took me for dinner to one of those large, oaky, muffled clubs which are the social zenith of English masculinity. When we entered the building, it seemed deserted save for a flat-chested and aged doorman. Descending into the depths, we left our hats and coats in a gloomy and abandoned cubby and then proceeded up a vast wide staircase to the dining-room where, in remote corners, three single diners, seated far apart, were bent to their food.

There were familiar things on the menu: roast beef, mutton, duck, ham.

And broiled bones!

I was too impressed even to enquire what in the Sam Hill broiled bones were. But, ever since, I have remembered them, and have kicked myself a thousand times for having failed to take them, instead of the vulgar roast beef.

Imagine my delight on entering a folksy New York restaurant with Ye Olde English style of exterior and interior décor to find broiled bones on the menu. I took 'em, with mounting excitement.

They were delicious. They were what we call spare ribs; only instead of pork ribs, they were beef. You take spare ribs, and I'll take broiled bones.

Learning

One of the beliefs very generally held by most of us a generation ago was that it was man's invention or discovery of fire that really started him on the way up from the brute beast.

It is known now that man had fire long ages before he had figured out any way of creating it by friction or spark. Fire was a commonplace wherever there was lightning to ignite it and the type of forest growth to nourish it. Some anthropologists are busy working on the theory that the more advanced tribes and early races of man were found in regions where there were good atmospheric and geographic conditions for forest fires – good lightning storms and good tindery forests – whereas the more backward races were found in jungles and deserts, where natural fire was not always at hand for man's use.

All primitive mythology is full of reference to "magic fire." I would suppose that for countless ages the smarter human tribes accepted lightning as a magic gift, and it was their sole source of fire. In my boyhood, I knew an old Indian named Solomon Aissance who told me that his grandfather was one of the two "fire carriers" of their tribe. I had imagined that all Indians knew how to make fire with rubbing sticks or flint and iron. But according to Solomon, the family fires in the tribe were not allowed to go out at any cost, and when the family or tribe moved, it was the duty of two old men to be "fire carriers" who transported living coals in clay pots carried on a litter. And their cunning was to know the woods that made the most durable coals for a day's journey.

It would be better for our pride if we continued to think that man had invented fire. But man has been given a great many breaks by nature, in his long history.

The chief difference between him and the brute creation is that he has been quick to see the breaks and grab them.

He saw a log floating down stream, and, seizing upon it, and thinking about it for six or seven thousand years, invented a boat.

And so on.

Give us time.

Shatterproof

The test of a good waiter or waitress comes when another one drops a tray-load of dishes with a shattering crash. The perfect waiter never turns a hair, never even glances in the direction of the disaster. With an aplomb unequalled by the late Queen Victoria or even Charles Laughton, the perfect waiter behaves not only as if nothing had happened but as though you were hearing things.

During the rush hour at lunch yesterday, in one of our busiest restaurants, a waitress, with a great tray-load of used dishes hoisted shoulder high, tripped on the foot of one of those gentlemen who can't sit at a table without contortions. There was a shrill scream followed by a slithering crash that brought a stunned silence over the room. The scream was not from the waitress but from a lady customer who saw the tray start on its descent.

Our waitress was in the act of pouring coffee from the thermos pitcher for one of us. She never even trembled. I glanced quickly about. All the waitresses were bending to their tables, taking orders, calmly at work at the serving tables.

"Did you hear something?" I asked our waitress.

"What?" said she.

It's part of their code.

<hr />

Leap Year (1960)

Don't make the mistake of thinking that this Leap Year business of permitting the girls to do the courting and proposing of marriage is one of these recent gimmicks like Mother's Day or beauty queens or onion week.

It goes back to very early times. A law was passed in Scotland in 1288 A.D. providing that any bachelor who turned down a proposal of marriage in Leap Year could be fined one pound, a sum much larger than it is today, and one that would make a Scotchman pause in any circumstances. Around that same era, laws governing the right of women to take the initiative in marriage proposal were in operation in many parts of Europe, and not in any spirit of jest at that.

For it has been recognized for centuries, especially in societies less complex than the present one, that not only were women at a great disadvantage in the whole process of marriage, but that there were men in every community who were even too shy, too undecided, or too plain calculating to face up to the problem of choosing a mate and settling down. Many and many a man, across the centuries, has been in the plight of a bachelor of my acquaintance who was so attractive to two women that he couldn't make up his mind which one to ask.

So finally, last Leap Year the bolder of the two women took the initiative. She proposed.

That decided him. He married the other.

The Stick

One of my summer cottage neighbours notices that during the summer, up at the lake, he does not need his glasses nearly as much as he does in town, during the working year.

He has often explained it to me.

"In the city," he says, "I spend eight hours a day in a confined space, in an office, where my normal focus is a matter of twenty or thirty feet down to two feet. My bifocals serve me well for that sort of life. But when I get up here to the cottage, in the wide open spaces, my eyes seem to relax, my vision expands. Except when I am doing something like painting a chair or carrying in stove wood, I hardly ever need my glasses."

Last week, he was walking fondly around his rocky premises, idly doing nothing, when he saw a stick lying on the ground, a dead branch, obviously, that had fallen off a tree.

"That branch," he said to himself, "looks exactly like a snake. It might give the women a start, if they come by ...."

He reached down and picked up the stick.

It was a snake.

He flung it, he says, about forty feet, by sheer sudden reflex action.

He wears his glasses all the time now.

The Damper

A lawyer friend of mine has the habit, familiar in most courtrooms, of addressing his own witnesses with great courtesy, and encouraging them to speak up. But a Jekyll and Hyde transformation comes over him when he assaults witnesses for his opposition. He shouts at them, and their replies, by contrast, sound muttered, timid, uncertain. For so many years has he followed these tactics that it has become an unconscious habit. It is automatic behaviour on his part.

I often go and sit in the spectators' enclosure when he is performing, just for the fun of it. It is good drama. The last time, I noticed among the waiting witnesses an old fishing crony of mine. During a brief recess, I met him out in the corridor having a smoke, and he told me he was not looking forward with much relish to being cross-examined by my lawyer friend.

"When he starts yelling at you," I advised, "look distressed, put your hand to your forehead, then turn and ask the judge to please request the lawyer to speak softly, as you have an ear ailment that causes you acute pain when people speak loudly."

This is precisely what he did. My lawyer friend was completely flummoxed. He was as confused as is an actor who forgets his lines. He muffed the cross-examination completely.

After court, when he and I were having a pot of tea together, he said:

"I don't know what's the matter with me today."

———❀———

The Shake-out

Unlike a dog, a cat will come straight up to a stranger and arch its back, stiffen its tail, and begin rubbing itself chummily against the newcomer's ankles. This is counted to the credit of cats. A dog, on the contrary, takes a dim view of strangers; sometimes barks and shows other signs of preliminary doubt and hostility; and it is only after a reasonable period of investigation that a dog will relax and admit of a friendly pat.

The effusive nature of cats is embarrassing to many people. And it may be for good reason. For a pet dealer informs me that the reason a cat comes so eagerly up to strangers and begins that business of rubbing its body so cosily against the ankles is simply that the cat is trying to get rid of its fleas. Notice, he says, how the cat fluffs out its fur so electrically when it is performing this act; how its body is stiffened and arched. Most people are not particularly receptive to cat fleas, and these are the people who receive the most enthusiastic welcome. If a cat jumps up on a stranger and appears to rejoice in crawling and snuggling, the stranger may reasonably assume that he or she has been recognized by the cat as one most likely to relieve it of some of its little troubles.

People who love animals are inclined to ascribe human motives to them, and to judge their behaviour by human standards. The scientists have a name for this; they call it anthropomorphism. Animals, however, are highly realistic and every advance in the study of their behaviour further convinces scientists that the basic principle of animal psychology is unenlightened self-interest. When a dog comes out of the water from a swim, it almost invariably tries to come near another dog or a person before shaking itself. The reason is said to be that the swim has disturbed the fleas on the dog, and it is in the hope of transferring some of its fleas onto a new host that the dog is so determined to shake itself in the immediate vicinity of another being, even its master or mistress. Animals obey very ancient rules of their tribe. So do human beings. One way or another, we are all eager to give our fleas to somebody else.

———✿———

This Town is Full of Strangers

There are many sensations to the business of growing older, many of them unpleasant. But the haunting one is the feeling of being a stranger in the place you knew so well.

In youth, if I remember, there is the feeling of being a stranger as you set out on your own into the formidable world. But most of us in a little while gather around us familiarities of people and place, and in the young prime of the thirties, we are very much at home in a world we love. The happier our forties and fifties, the more we love the familiar world, and there are no strangers in it, least of all ourselves. But somewhere in our sixties, family and friends begin quietly to drop away. For a while we don't notice that we are becoming surrounded by strangers. Then it occurs to us that the place which we have known so long isn't the same. The streets have changed. Tall buildings full of strangeness where there were short buildings, familiar as our hat on the doorknob. We hurry home.

The sights change, the sounds change, the pace changes, the young speak an alien tongue. As if by stealth, the realization comes to us that we are strangers in the place we thought we knew so well. It is an eerie feeling.

Shifty

While some rascals don't look like rascals at all, but like deacons, the general rule is that a shifty individual looks shifty, male or female. Why, then, do people do business with obviously shifty characters?

The answer may be that those who do business with shifty individuals are looking for a little fraudulent advantage or even illegal profit, and are therefore a little shifty themselves. An acquaintance of mine has been complaining bitterly about a suit of clothes he bought recently which, in less than a month's wear, lost its shape and began falling apart in the way cheaply made clothes do. From one of the business confrères, I learned that he had been involved in an accident at the plant in which his clothes were damaged, and his employer had told him to buy a new suit and charge it to the firm.

After shopping around, he found a shifty gentleman in the clothes trade who agreed to sell him a suit for $45 and give him a bill for $75.

Naturally, the shifty gentleman sold him a $35-suit. Which accounts for the necessary indignation of the buyer, who has to appear to be outraged that a $75-suit should look so bad so soon.

———— ❁ ————

The Upsetter

One of our women friends says she has the worst luck.

She is always breaking the handles off tea cups, upsetting jugs in the fridge, letting food burn in the oven.

She is the kind of person who, if you let her in your rowboat in summer, will step on your fishing rods for sure. If the bus goes by her house every six minutes, she will just come out the front door as it passes, and the bus stop only a hundred feet away.

And it's raining.

If she buys tickets for the ballet or theatre for a Tuesday night, she will think it is for Wednesday, and not find out until she arrives at the theatre door.

Last night, when she and her husband arrived at our house, she had lost her purse. It wasn't in their car. It wasn't at the restaurant where they had eaten supper. The husband phoned there, and tried to get a couple of shops they had visited before six.

"I have the worst luck!" she reiterated, when her husband came wearily from the telephone.

"You're just careless," said he.

"I am not!" she protested hotly. "Maybe it's my eyesight."

"Or," I suggested mildly, thinking of my poor fishing rods and all those cups with their handles off and those dishes upset in the fridge, "maybe it is just poor co-ordination. Reflexes, or something."

She looked at me gratefully.

"Careless," repeated her husband firmly. "You just don't pay attention to what you're doing."

When her husband and I went to the kitchen to put the kettle on and slice some Spanish onions for sandwiches, he shut the door and faced me.

"Not unlucky," he said. "Not careless. Not eyesight. Not reflexes. Just plain lazy!"

There may be something in it. He ought to know.

Collie

A collie dog of my acquaintance is the most royal and serene character you ever saw whenever all the family to which he belongs is gathered on the cottage verandah, with nobody absent, and with each adult and child sitting in full view and at rest.

The instinct to herd is an overpowering passion in a collie. As his ancestors for timeless generations herded and tended the sheep, so the collie today herds his human flock, and is restless and unhappy when they stray.

When the family moves down off the verandah to the cottage wharf for the afternoon swim, the collie's anxiety reaches the bursting point. He barks, leaps about excitedly, and emits warning whines. When the children dive into the treacherous water and scatter out all over the landscape like strayed lambs, the collie gallops up and down, barking, protesting, whining, signalling the safe way home. Strangers imagine he is just a noisy dog at such times. But he is simply being a collie.

After a while, when the swimmers grow less frisky and return to the wharf to sunbathe, the collie runs about, checking, counting, and making sure all are safe and sound. When they relax and settle down and stay put, the collie, after one final census, sighs heavily and sinks down with a thud on the dock, rests his long muzzle on his paws, and dotes upon the flock, safely garnered, safely herded.

And finally, at last, when the family, full of swimming and sunbathed enough, get up and wander back to the house, the collie, all radiant with relief, leads them up to the beach and onto the verandah. This is the fold. This is the "bucht," as the shepherds call it.

And so for a little while, his job is done. And were you to pass by and see his tawny majesty lying couchant on the verandah, you might never know what comfort is in his heart.

The Big Think

Referring to a scholar of some distinction, one of his colleagues said:

"He has a mind like one of those IBM computers. It contains nothing but what has been fed into it."

The scholarly mind is being put to a spectacular test nowadays. So swift has been the rising tide of sheer detail in the recent past that the question is asked: How much can the human mind hold and still leave room for thinking? In most scientific areas, it takes half a dozen scientists to face up to a given question. It is like the famous tall pine tree in the Paul Bunyan legend. It took five men all looking at it at the same time to see the top of it.

I had lunch with three scholars the other noon. I was spellbound by their erudition. But one had forgotten his wallet. One had shaved only one side of his face that morning. And the other didn't remember until we were leaving the restaurant that he was supposed to have lunch with his wife.

Pest Control

One of the advantages of going a little deaf is that you no longer hear the mosquitoes. It was hearing the threatening zing of the mosquito, as you lay in bed after turning out the light, that was the infuriating feature of the pest.

You turned out the light and snuggled around to find the most comfortable part of the mattress in the summer cottage or resort bed. You relaxed and reviewed pleasantly the experiences of the day and the prospects of the morrow. And then "peeeeeeennnnnn!"

There it was. You hid your hands under the sheet, keeping one handy to make a quick slap when the creature landed on your only exposed surface, your face. It came near. It retreated. It went round and round. No longer relaxed, you were as tense as a gun spring. The beast went far away, up to the ceiling. Then down past your ear.

If only it would land!

But when you begin to lose your hearing, you are spared all that agony. Something tiny lands on your forehead. You slap.

That's it. You go to sleep.

⎯⎯⎯⎯✿⎯⎯⎯⎯

Turn in Your Old Name

The rumour is that some of our ancestors, on arriving in this country, changed their names. They doubtless had practical reasons for doing so. But there is a sentimental reason why a good many Canadians ought to change their family names. A deed poll costs only a few dollars. And most judges are not particular about the reasons a man submits for changing his name, so long as it is an honest one.

And the most honest reason in the world a man could offer is his love of Canada, or the village, township or neighbourhood from which he and his family come. The family names we bear now are not particularly hallowed by antiquity. Most of them are only three hundred years old, more or less. There are some among us who like to trace their names back to the Domesday Book, not reflecting that most of those names were given to our English ancestors off-hand, by their French conquerors on the spur of the moment. Some of us were named, from time to time, by our trade, like smith, clerk, fletcher, tailor. But most of us got our family names from the village or place from which we came. And since we moved about from generation to generation, no doubt our ancestors bore various names in various generations. The son of a smith, moreover, might become a tailor. Our family names are not half as important as we assume them to be. Then why not, by deed poll, begin adopting family names associated with our own now well-founded country?

There are families that have lived two centuries on the Restigouche and Mirimichi Rivers. British Columbia abounds in the loveliest place and river names. In Ontario, where most of the settlers were apparently homesick, the rivers are the Thames, the Humber, the Trent, and so on. But Ontario still glories in such village names as Omemee, Nipissing, Biscotasing. If some long-established and fashionable Canadian family of some such name as Gilch would start the ball rolling, I imagine many of us would follow.

⎯⎯❋⎯⎯

Fire in August

It is true that lightning is responsible for a great many fires. But human carelessness with camp and picnic fires, with cigarette butts tossed from car and truck windows is responsible for so many millions of dollars expended in fighting that the fury of a tired fire ranger at the end of one of his battles is easily understood.

A fire ranger friend of mine overtook a camping party of two men and two women who were standing on the shore in quiet rage at the sight that met their eyes. One of the most beautiful campsites in the region had been burned out the previous year by careless campers who had failed to extinguish the fire in the open-air stone fireplace the campsite afforded. The ranger pulled his boat in alongside them.

"Isn't that a dreadful sight!" cried one of the tourists. "Why, for three years past, we have camped here every trip.

And we have always remembered this spot as the highlight of our whole holiday. You know how you feel about certain spots?"

The ranger admitted he did indeed.

"Why, last year," said one of the shocked women, "we camped here for three days. It was a lovely August, last year."

"What time in August were you here?" asked the ranger.

And before the men could stop her, the woman said:

"I can tell you exactly. We were here the ninth, tenth, and eleventh of August. We left the afternoon of the eleventh ..."

Then she caught her husband's eye and cut off as if she had bitten her tongue.

The ranger grimly drew a little hip-flattened notebook from his pocket and flipped its pages.

"The fire," he said, "that burnt this point occurred last year on the late afternoon of the eleventh of August."

Uncle Pete's Affliction

My uncle Pete was troubled all his life with insomnia. He could never sleep at night. He tossed and turned, groaned and muttered, and would get up, every few hours, to stand and stare out the windows at the ruthless night, usually tripping over a chair or banging into the half-open bedroom door in the process, thus startling everybody else out of their honest sleep.

The reason Uncle Pete couldn't sleep at night was that he usually slept half the day.

Pete was one of those fellows who loved to hear people

talk, because he could lean back in his chair and doze the while. Sitting at a desk, he could rest his chin in his hand and his elbow on the desk, and waft away into sweet dreamland. It was his firm belief that after lunch, a man should lie down for forty winks. He quoted the great Churchill on this. Churchill, he said, owed his boundless vitality to the fact that after every meal, he lay down for a quick nip of slumber.

Uncle Pete never went for a motor ride that he didn't get in the back seat, and, in five minutes, with the purr of the engine, be away. He loved to go to movies, especially in the afternoon. I doubt if he ever saw a complete movie in his entire life.

In the family, he was reputed as a great churchgoer. It was wonderful to see him sitting there, bolt upright, his eyes downcast in piety. It was fun to see him flounder to his feet when the last hymn was announced and the organ burst forth.

But he was a martyr. He had insomnia. He couldn't sleep at night.

Water

Apart from desiring to get his arms around his loved ones at home, the most familiar of all yearnings of a soldier in the most recent great war was for a tap, running clear, cold Canadian water.

What he dreamed of, as he stood in the muggy cold of an English dawn, with an ugly tin basin – it was more of a miniature tub – full of tepid water, was a beautiful bathroom, with a dry floor underfoot, and a clean white basin, with two gushing taps, answering the mere twist of his fingers. In the sour chill of the Italian daybreak, as he shared with his mates the scummy pails of suspect well-water from the fountains of Bandusia that Horace sang, he fairly ached with the memory of the fragrant bathtubs of home.

With a scabby glass of the true, the blushful Hippocrene to his lips – though white or red it was only *vino* at about four cents the bucket – he gagged slightly as a vision of the old familiar kitchen of home, and the sink and the tap, brass or chrome, bending humbly over it came to mind. And out of the tap in memory flowing a nectar all the gods of Rome never knew – cold, sweet Canadian water.

It is a thing we forget, until we are far away, that nothing tastes so sweet, nothing hits the spot, nothing comes so close to being of the essence of home as the water out of the kitchen tap.

In Normandy in a ditch I came upon a youngster with a bullet in the thick of his leg and we sat with him until the motor ambulance came along. He was terribly thirsty, and as he emptied our water bottles as well as his own, he sighed: "All I want is a frosty glassful of water out of our pump at the farm back home."

I feel sure he got it. And I hope he always thinks how good it tastes.

A Useful Word, Intuitably

Here I have been writing words for fifty years and never knew until yesterday that there was a word intuit.

I have known the word intuition all my life. I can recall my old classics master, David Alexander Glassey, accusing me of trying to translate Xenophon by intuition instead of by studying my vocabulary and Greek grammar. Later, I served under editors who declared that I covered a news event by intuition rather than by digging out the facts. Intuition, I knew, meant the direct perception of truth, facts, and so on, independent of any reasoning process. It's a very handy faculty, if you can get away with it.

But here is this word intuit. It is pronounced exactly like into-it. I intuit. I do not reason, I intuit! What a dandy word. I intuit, you intuit, he intuits. I intuited it, you intuited it, he intuited it. There's the grammar of it and a little Eskimoan it sounds.

"The way I intuit it," you say calmly, avoiding all statistics, and confounding your hearers, "is . . ."

I have needed this word for years.

The Guest

On my travels, I stopped at a particularly comfortable hotel, quiet, mannerly, immaculately clean. Its dining-room was an old-fashioned delight, and unlike almost all modern dining-rooms, it invited you to linger over your meal. In my visits to the dining room I was particularly struck by an elderly couple who sat at the same table in a corner each day. They seemed to be special guests. They appeared to be given VIP treatment.

I liked the old man, a short, fat gourmet who chewed his food slowly and thoughtfully, rolling his eyes from time to time, and pausing, while chewing, to take deep appreciative breaths through his nose. I asked the captain of waiters who he was.

"Oh, he's the owner," said the captain. "He was a very prosperous businessman, and when he retired and sold out his business, he bought the hotel so he and his wife could live in comfort the rest of their lives. No trouble over domestic help. Lovely apartment. Good food. Hundred per cent service. Beautiful garden. The hotel gives him ten per cent on his investment, and he never gets a hotel bill."

"Does he take a hand in the management?" I asked.

"Oh, dear no!" said the captain. "Strictly a guest."

Unfiltered

One of the most addicted cigarette smokers among my acquaintances has for years past used a cigarette holder that has a patented filter in it. Small tubes containing tiny white crystals are inserted into the holder daily, or oftener. And when the smoker changes the filter, it comes out as brown and shiny as a date. This proves to him that he is missing the tars and nicotine the advertisers refer to.

Recently he tried a double gimmick. He smoked filter cigarettes in his filter holder. And you can imagine his astonishment when he found that his crystal filters came out as brown as usual. He at once wrote the filter cigarette people, but they didn't answer him.

For some reason all this reminds me of my childhood and the numerous gentlemen of worth and social standing who chewed tobacco. Now, if there is any way you can get the full value of the tars and nicotines in tobacco, it must be by biting off a hunk of blackstrap chewing tobacco from the plug and tucking it in behind your molars for a good long soak. Among those I knew well who enjoyed this fatal habit were university professors, medical doctors, general managers of large implement factories, colonels of regiments, and one presbyterian minister, all of whom lived to ripe old age and died, as you might say, in good health.

The Meddler

An acquaintance of mine by the name of John Macintyre has just reached the age at which a fellow discovers, to his astonishment, that there is a language, and that all those sounds his elders have been making each has a meaning. He has encountered a little difficulty in shaping his mouth and tongue to the exact contortions required by some of the sounds uttered by others. For example, one of his first experiments was with his own name. Macintyre is not the easiest of names to pronounce, as are Smiff, Clark, Bwown and so on. It came out as Johnnie McTawda, which is very good, considering. In fact, to the ears of many of his friends and family, including myself, it is a better name than John Macintyre.

Johnnie McTawda. Among his favourite words is mushpuppy, which I think accurately describes one of Johnnie McTawda's favourite eatables, to wit, marshmallows. From the point of view of semantics, mushpuppy conveys the idea of a marshmallow far better than does the word marshmallow. If you said "Pass the mushpuppies" to an Eskimo, he would most likely know what you meant and would pass the mushpuppies.

Last week, Johnnie McTawda came into the kitchen and faced his Grandma McTawda.

"Marsh," he enunciated solemnly, "mallow!"

"Who told you to say that!" cried his grief-stricken grandma.

"Unk," said Johnnie McTawda, referring to the elderly gentleman who lives next door.

The entire Macintyre clan, together with all their friends, are now wishing Unk boils, blisters, and bunions.

Apples

Everybody, and I mean the rich and the poor, the little back street cottages and the mansions on the hill, used to buy a couple of barrels of apples about the end of September. A barrel of greenings and a barrel of spies, or a barrel of red astrachans and a barrel of pippins. I speak of fifty years ago.

The barrels were kept either in the cellar or in the back kitchen. They cost a couple of dollars a barrel. If you had relatives in the country, and fifty years ago nearly everybody had relatives in the country, you often got them for a dollar and a half a barrel, and maybe as gifts.

Apples, I suppose, were our vitamins in those days, long before the intrusion of cold storage, in the days when oranges were Christmas, and the fresh vegetables were the cabbages, parsnips from the farmers' root cellars.

If they were kept in the back kitchen, as they were in my home, they lent a savoury atmosphere to the back door entrance that was as characteristic of home as the warm spicy odour of grandma's cookies, which were cooked not once a week, but, in the strange shortening of memories, nearly every day. If in the cellar, the redolent apples greeted you as you opened the cellar stairway door, though they were fifteen steps down and thirty steps in to the fruit cellar, up front.

But the thing about apples that puzzles me now is – how they kept. Were our furnaces weaker than they are today? Have back kitchens, unheated, gone forever? For if we buy so much as a measly bushel of spies today, they are punky in ten days, and gone in two weeks. We have to buy apples by the pound now. They will be in the fruit stores all winter, coming from cold storage, but you buy them by the pound, or the dozen, and eat them without delay.

A farmer friend of mine, who still keeps the apples of his own orchard in barrels in his own back kitchen, says that it is not altogether a question of the temperature of modern living. It may be that modern methods of growing apples, the fertilizers used to produce pretty apples, big apples, the sprays, the handling, may have something to do with the change in the sturdiness of apples.

"They're improved," he says. "Everything you get in cities is improved, so I hear."

The Health Hazard

An old schoolmate of mine, now in his sixties, has had a successful business career despite a horrible habit he had as a boy and which he has preserved to this day.

You meet him on the street, and, sure as fate, after the casual greeting, he suddenly looks acutely into your face and says:

"Say, you're not looking too well. Anything wrong?"

Or, another favourite of his:

"You're looking tired, old man. Tired out."

In his youth, it was the same thing. Many a husky rugby player had the gimp knocked out of him by these solicitous enquiries, the morning of the game.

On the bus yesterday, he gave me the usual kindly enquiry: I didn't look too well.

"Well," I said, "you don't look too well yourself. You look sort of shrivelled. How old are you now, Wesley? You must have lost ten pounds since I last saw you. Why don't you take a holiday?"

Wesley's wife phoned me last night. She's an old schoolmate too.

"What on earth have you said to Wesley?" she stormed. "He's gone to bed, almost in a collapse. He said you ..."

I explained I had merely been giving Wesley back some of his own line.

So I am a brute. But feeling much better.

Hepatica

The general resurrection of nature in spring is the subject of wonder and delight in every gardener and in everybody who can find time to glance about for a moment at all the less aggressive creatures who share with us, for a little while, the mystery of life. We go to the most costly and elaborate precautions to keep ourselves alive over the winter. We live in a regular fortress of civilization against winter.

And then we go out to a well-known spot in some wood-lot, where last April and other Aprils before we found a fragile hepatica blooming. At the floor of a particular tree. And there, sure enough, it is again. Or still.

Its roots have been encased in solid ice all winter; its half-evergreen foliage has been heaped with snow, pelted with sleet, frozen, lashed, blasted by blizzards. But out of the mud, on soft stems, lift up the indescribably delicate flowers as sure as fate. None of us can guess how many centuries, how many hundreds of centuries, this same plant has calmly flourished in this very spot, renewing itself forever. The thought of its fragility, its personal carelessness and its eternity is enough to send us hurrying home to our fortress pursued by a shadowing sense of our own transience.

How valiantly we have survived winter, with billions upon billions of dollars' worth of organized shelter, food, heat, light, clothing, transportation, and entertainment to keep us happy. And then, lifting our eyes from the hepatica, we behold in the slanting April sunlight a cloud of midges dancing. So small, so insignificant, mere animate dust. Where have they been all winter? How in heaven's name did they survive?

It is man that is fragile. How he has survived this long must be a puzzle to all else in nature.

Mr. Foosh

My neighbour, Mr. Foosh, a Scotsman, naturally, with a name like that, had a curious experience whilst cleaning his rather complicated teeth. The dentifrice, he discovered, had a most curious taste. Mr. Foosh is elderly and slightly addicted to the grape, as the saying is, with the full concurrence of his medical adviser, a Doctor Hector MacSwivell, who believes a moderate application of alcohol to the veins and arteries restores something of their elasticity that may have been lost through advancing age. Mr. Foosh, as I was saying, not infrequently notices a curious flavour to almost everything first thing in the morning. He is used to it.

But this dentifrice, he decided, had reached the end of its popularity with him. He would have to try a new one. After he had finished his teeth, he picked up the tube to read its name so as to be sure not to buy it again. It was then he discovered that he had inadvertently squeezed a tube of household cement onto his brush, his daughter having left the tube in the bathroom after repairing one of her earrings which had come unstuck.

Mr. Foosh was relating these details to me as we boarded the bus, and my sympathetic attention was so distracted that I threw away my bus ticket and put my cigarette butt in the ticket receptacle. After a certain age, it becomes difficult to keep things in order.

Stumped

A small boy of six, listening to his two uncles exchanging war reminiscences, became horror-struck. In the familiar half-humorous style in which soldiers relate their blood-thirstiest experiences, full of understatement and almost amiable references to death and destruction, the two veterans, all unconscious of their infant audience, went through their familiar routine.

Then the small boy squeezed his way between them.

"Uncle Tommie," said he, "why do men kill each other when there are little boys in them?"

"How's that?" asked Uncle Tommie.

"When a man grows up," said the child, "he used to be a little boy. So when you kill a man you kill a little boy too."

The two uncles looked awkwardly at each other.

"What do you say," they cried, "let's get our coats on and drive over to the corner for some ice cream, hey?"

And in a great remorseful scramble, they tried to erase from the child's mind the question they could not answer, and indeed had never thought of.

For what does happen to the child that is in us all, that lovely thing, aged four, six, eight, around which has grown, year by year, the fungus of time?

June Bug

In my neighbour's garden over the fence, I saw an heroic battle between a June bug and a dachshund. Being myself highly susceptible to the terrors of June bugs, especially in the gloaming, or after dark has fallen, and they come zooming like buzz bombs straight for your hair, I was able to appreciate the sentiments of the dachshund when he discovered in the grass this chocolate monster, though it was broad daylight.

I take into consideration the fact that the dachshund's soft underbelly is only two inches off the ground. And what must a dachshund's reaction be to see, fair in his path, staggering on six horrid spiny legs, this polished spectre? Why, four more steps, and the dachshund would have been half-way over it!

What caught my attention was the sight of the little dog pointing his slender nose straight at the ground, ears laid back, and long body slowly arching in horror. Up, up arched the back until the belly was a good six inches free of the grass. Then, with wild barks that grew hysterical, and spinning round and round in circles with his nose for a pivot, the dog called upon all humanity to come running.

Nobody came. The June bug continued to stagger his blind way amid the grass. The dog went crazy. He began snapping, but always at a safe distance, showing an almost human-like reluctance to come truly to grips with the monstrous brown beetle. Then the June bug took wing and flew off.

Picking his way carefully, eyeing the grass in front of him and all around, the dachshund withdrew, belly tucked up, to the flagstone patio, sniffed thoroughly the bare stone, and most cautiously sat down.

Everything Gets Fragile

One thing I have noticed since I started walking the plank which extends from a man's sixtieth to his seventieth year is that I have begun to knock things over.

When I reach for my toothbrush in the morning, I upset a bottle of my wife's hand lotion beside it in the medicine chest. The tea caddy is up on the second shelf of one of the kitchen cupboards. I get the tea caddy, all right, but down comes a bottle of Worcestershire sauce too. Turning on a table-lamp is no trick. I've done it automatically millions of times. You just walk over, reach up under the lamp's kilts, feel for the little push button and push it. That's all there is to it. But lately I am disturbed to discover how tottery table-lamps can get. The darn things topple over at practically a touch. Mark you: this is the same old lamp I have been turning on for years and years. But I suppose as a lamp grows older, it begins to lose its fine sense of balance.

Tea cups, for another thing, have become steadily more unreliable and shaky in the past few years. I refer to the older style of cups. I am happy to observe that the china and ceramics industry has recognized this fact too, and within recent years has been turning out larger and larger quantities of good thick mugs, and tea cups of stout peasant ware. They don't shake quite so much as the old style of china cups, and if you do knock them over, they break much more quietly and with less ostentation.

Now that I come to think of it, a great many things around the house have in quite recent years lost much of the stability that formerly characterized them. The balance of those little nesting tables that you distribute around the room when company calls used to be remarkable. But I suppose walnut suffers from senility like anything else. These little tables tumble all over the place of late years. Pipes in the pipe rack, even my tobacco tins, don't seem to be made of the sturdy, solid stuff they formerly were. They're flimsy. They skid and slither as you reach for them.

One thing I will say, though, about walking that plank between the years of sixty and seventy. You become very tolerant with regard to the instability and faithlessness of those formerly faithful old friends and servants.

And another thing: you don't grab when they totter and fall.

You just let the darn things drop.

The Phrenologist

On TV the other night I saw a phrenologist and heard him expounding the principles of this interesting subject. I hadn't even heard of a phrenologist for years. Psychologists have pushed them right off the map.

But when I was a boy, phrenologists were just as much a part of the local landscape as psychiatrists and IQ experts are today. In fact, in the shopping block less than two streets from my childhood home there were two phrenologists doing a thriving business. The old-fashioned one, whom most of the mothers in the neighbourhood had faith in, occupied a store. In its window was a large four-foot poster, showing the human head, cut in half like a physiology chart, and showing that gruesome gob of fishworms with which our skulls are filled, and all the bumps, from the size and shape of which the delicate-handed phrenologist could read our characters, define our "faculties," and advise our mothers what to expect of us when we grew up. The new-fangled phrenologist, further up the street, had an office over a hardware store, just like a doctor.

Midway between the two was the big store owned by another distinguished practitioner who employed the title Doctor and he dealt exclusively in tapeworms. His shop window was full of tall bottles and short bottles filled with pallid white pickled tapeworms, some of them forty feet long and an inch wide. The labels told the names and addresses of the fortunate ones who had been liberated from these monsters.

The old phrenologist "did" me, and told my mother all my faculties pointed to a distinguished career in banking and finance.

I had failed to tell my mother, and I did not tell the Professor that the lump on my head was from Jack Calder, who hit me with a baseball bat at recess.

Teresa

When we speak of the younger generation, we have to be careful of that generalization. Maybe there is no such thing. There was a matinee at O'Keefe Centre in Toronto of the opera *Madame Butterfly*, which, instead of the usual curtain rise of 2:30, did not begin until 4:00 P.M. and ran well towards 7:00 P.M. It was presented specially for the school children of the metropolitan region, and of the thirty-two hundred seats in the huge theatre, somewhere between a thousand and two thousand were occupied by the younger generation.

We older members of the audience were a little uneasy in such ebullient company. But when the theatre darkened and the prelude began, there was instant silence. I doubt if Teresa Stratas will often have so still an audience. Children must breathe more softly than do we elders. Composers of opera leave a space, at the end of the great arias, the orchestra stops, and the prima donna bows in expectation of her traditional applause. When Teresa Stratas stood so bowed at the end of her first aria, after coming with her procession across the little bridge, she faced total and absolute silence. She raised her eyes. And we old people, whose poised hands were paralyzed by that stillness, knew that Stratas knew. She had bewitched two thousand teenagers. From there on, she sang as one bewitched, too, and to thunderous applause at each curtain. They were a magnificent audience, the younger generation.

Middle Age:
The Spaced Out Season

At a recent small gathering of people, mostly in their sixties, with a few in their seventies, one of the speakers said:

"For middle-aged people like us ..."

And there was neither a snort nor a snicker from the entire company.

Middle-aged? What is middle-aged? I went to the public library and consulted all the dictionaries, both large and small. And not one of them would take a chance on a definition of middle-aged. They skirted cautiously all around the term. "Neither young nor old," said one dictionary. "Of middle age," said another evasively, "between youth and old age."

So I turned to the doctors and called up three or four of my acquaintance. "Forty," said one doctor, "to fifty-five." Another set middle age at thirty-five to fifty.

"From the medical standpoint," said he, "you are no longer young at thirty-five, and at fifty, you have begun to get old."

But one of the doctors was as sly as the dictionaries.

"It's all how you feel," he said. "Some people are middle-aged at thirty, and others are still middle-aged at close to seventy."

In other words, middle-aged doesn't mean much of anything.

A Word for the Wolf

Every time I write or speak about wolves, I get into quite a ruckus with those whose hatred of the wolf is implacable. My own feeling is that if there were to be a hydrogen bomb explosion that wiped out practically all life on this sizzling little planet, two creatures might stand a slight chance of survival. And they are man and wolf. Both are clever, crafty, cunning, and gifted with the will to survive.

Maybe the widespread hatred of the wolf, which goes back into the history and folklore of nearly every nation, is due to the fact that the wolf is a high-level competitor. If little girls hate wolves because of Little Red Riding Hood, you will find any number of backwoodsmen, trappers, hunters, and sportsmen, who hate him because he is elusive, destructive, and perennial. The hand of man has been against the wolf now on this continent for somewhere near five hundred years in ever-growing enmity. Guns, traps, and poison have been used against him. The backwoods settler hates him because he kills sheep and calves. The trapper fights him because he destroys pelts in the traps. The sportsman joins the hue and cry because the wolf destroys large numbers of deer that the sportsman wants himself. He hasn't a friend. Yet let the hue and cry die down for only a little while, and suddenly, in the distance, as night falls and the moon comes up, you hear the spine-chilling wail of the wolf on a far hill.

I have no interest in trying to work up sympathy for the wolf. All I think we should do is respect him a little more highly than we do. He's quite a character, if for no other reason than that he has survived the hostility of man when so many other creatures have failed to do so.

Acquaintance

What is the difference between a friend and an acquaintance?

An elderly lady of my acquaintance has this definition:

"A friend is anyone who can drop in any old time and stay for breakfast, lunch, or supper, and no fuss. An acquaintance is somebody you have to invite."

The way she says invite, you envisage all sorts of preparation. The whole house has to be dusted and tidied and polished (for fear the acquaintance might wander around). A meal has to be planned and prepared. You have to dress up.

In short, acquaintances are something of a nuisance.

"Then," I enquired, "what do you do if an acquaintance drops in about eleven-thirty in the morning or around five in the afternoon?"

"You just sit it out," said my acquaintance.

So we just sat it out. When it became a quarter to six, she was beginning to take deep breaths and glance out the window rather pointedly, and our conversation, even on points of etiquette and what is called semantics (a most fascinating subject) was growing desultory, I finally got around to what I had called for.

"How," I suggested, "about coming with me to a little joint I have discovered where some Hungarians have set up a little dining-room and they serve a thing called ..."

She did not even wait to hear what it is called, but was hustling upstairs to put on the finery reserved, usually, for acquaintances.

Old (sad) Thrills

In some consternation, I watched my small grandchildren squatted before the TV, glued to a western in which villains were dying in bunches, Indians were biting the dust, and ferocity was rampant in raging cayuses and stage coaches swerving on the edges of precipices.

I tried to hark back in memory to the time I was the age of these children, and to recollect what forces played upon my infant emotions and sensibilities. We had uncles who told ghost stories that chilled our marrow. But the uncles were fat and jovial men who smoked cigars, and we knew even in our marrows that there were no ghosts. Among our aunties there was always one who sang contralto, and she had the sad songs to sing. With us gathered around the piano, she would dolefully intone:

> Into the tent where a
> gypsy boy lay
> Dying alone at the close
> of the day . . .

There was another about a Little Boy Blue who heard not the sounds of alarm and would never come back to the farm. We wept for them, and our elders wept for the bird in the gilded cage.

I was fogbound in these memories when the western ended, and my grandchildren leaped to their feet with a tear for nobody.

Disjointed

The attention the medical and surgical professions are paying to the heart, brain, liver, lungs, and other giblets, seems to me to be misplaced. They should be concentrating on the joints. It is in the joints we go first.

This past summer, I leaped lightly into my outboard skiff in a fashion I have practised for sixty-four years. My heart is still good. My brain is as clear as ever. No liver spots dance before my eyes. My lungs suck deep and pure. But the way I landed in the skiff, it was a mercy nobody was looking. My joints just failed to act. Not only my ankles, knees and hip bones, but that main swivel joint in the small of the back, which you might call the main joint, all collapsed, and, somewhat like a roll of old carpet, I sagged onto the bottom of the skiff, the larger half of me suspended over the gunwale. And when I commanded my joints to step lively to save us all from going overboard, they just refused. So over we went, slow and without fuss, brain, heart, liver, lungs, joints and all.

The reason I speak of what formerly were component parts of a whole as if they were separate entities is in accordance with the trend in modern medicine. We have specialists now who deal with only one organ in what used to be a single organism. We have heart specialists, brain specialists, lung specialists, and so on. It is hard for us laymen not to conceive that we are incorporated companies rather than individuals. And the older we get, the stronger grows that conception. In bygone days, we spoke of "my heart," "my lungs," "my liver." Not any more. You meet a man on the street and say "how are you?" and he immediately refers to "the heart," "the lungs," "the liver," as if he were speaking of fellow employees.

"The old ticker," says your friend, "has been acting up."

It is as if the ticker were disembodied.

That is precisely the way I feel about my joints, and I suggest the medical men wake up to the fact that it is in the joints we go first. You can see it all around you. On the street, in the office, at home. The way they step off the curb when the traffic lights change. Everybody over forty goes clunk. The way they get on the bus or train. Everybody over forty appears to be constructed of Meccano. Just watch anybody over forty, even your loved ones, going upstairs.

Joints, gentlemen, the joints. How do we prevent them assuming an air of privacy apart from us?

Reserves

A doctor friend of mine, who owns one of those expensive air rifles, is a chum of the police chief, and hates starlings, looked out his bathroom window whilst shaving the other morning and saw two starlings sitting on the telephone wire across his side drive.

Last year, too late, the doctor discovered that starlings had nested in his eaves troughs and caused all sorts of trouble.

Suspecting the intentions of these two birds on the wire, who were talking animatedly to each other, the doctor slipped away and got his air rifle and plinked one of the birds. The other flew off.

The doctor continued his shave, and half-way through, glancing out the window, he saw two starlings in exactly the same spot as they had been. Glancing down, he saw a dead starling in the side drive. So he had not missed. Taking aim, the doctor plinked another of the pair, and the survivor flew off.

Less than five minutes later, drying his hands, the doctor saw, to his consternation, two more starlings billing and cooing, if you can call the starling chatter cooing, in precisely the same spot as previously. He plinked another, the survivor flying off.

Half-way through breakfast, he could not resist running upstairs, and sure enough, there was another pair, on the same wire, in the same spot. So the doctor sneaked to the front of the house, climbed out on the verandah roof, and, taking a flanking shot, succeeded in downing both birds with the one pellet.

"No darn starlings," he said, rather ruefully looking down at all the little peaceful bodies strewn on his side drive, "are going to plug my eaves troughs this year!"

He finished his breakfast with appetite not entirely undisturbed, and went out to pick up the victims, to put in the garbage. Something caught his eye aloft. Two starlings were sitting, in conjugal discourse, on the telephone wire in precisely the same spot over his side drive.

"What did you do?" I enquired of the doctor.

"I gave up," he said. "I might better shoot snowflakes to drive away winter."

Now he has got two starlings in his eaves troughs.

<hr />

Downside of the Year

Around the middle of August there comes an instant, a fleeting flash of insight for all of us, in which we realize that the turn of the year has come, that summer is closing, and that autumn is at the door. In June, we imagine the summer ahead of us is a long, long season that may, indeed, never end. In June, we have completely forgotten September. In July, the lovely impression of floating in time remains with us. It is for this, we say, that the year is made. Even in the first week or two of August, the illusion of the continuance of summer lingers in our minds.

But without warning, and usually on a particularly fine August day, there comes this sudden melancholy instant of realization. It passes as instantly as it comes. It is like a flick of intimation. And we perceive for the first time since June, that we are on the downhill side of the year.

How quickly now the days and few remaining weeks will tumble down the hill. It is as if we had received a warning and from now on we will be alert to the shortening days, the earlier nightfall, the gathering hale winds; we will be conscious of the heaviness of the foliage in the trees. The yellows and purples of goldenrod and wild aster will assert themselves to our eyes, accustomed to the greens and blues of summer, and we will know it is time to wake up from the dream and get ready for the long reality that lies between September and next May.

———✸———

Mad

In the matter of courtesy, we can apparently overdo it with elderly women. Times have changed. Just as I entered a revolving door in one of the big stores, I noted a little old lady about to nip in on her side of it. The door was spinning just a trifle fast. As I stepped in, I took hold of the bar and set my posterior against the rear panel to slow it down.

The old lady nipped in. She gave me an indignant glance. And with a strength that struck me as astonishing, she gave the door a solid shove that sent me practically sprawling out my side. I looked back. She had set the door really to spinning, and had emerged very nimbly out onto the street. She too was looking back, at me. First, she glared. Then in response to my astonished expression, she impulsively grinned. Since it is the newspaperman's duty to investigate all phenomena, I stepped back into the revolving door and came out to her, lifting my hat politely.

"Sorry," said she contritely.

"You mad about something?" I enquired.

"Yes I am!" she stated emphatically, shifting her parcels in her arms. "I came downtown shopping this morning. And everybody has been treating me as if I were a helpless old woman!"

She stared at me a moment, in challenge. I held my face steady, for she really was a rather frail old party.

"That darn bus driver," she said, "got up out of his seat to help me onto the bus. A middle-aged woman jumped up to give me her seat. I went first to the glove counter. And what does the girl do? She hurries and gets a chair for me to sit on. It's been like that all morning. Everybody hopping around, making room for me, taking my elbow ... And then you slow down the door for me!"

"It was going too fast for me," I submitted.

She gave me a sly smile.

"I felt fine when I got up this morning," she said. "Haven't felt better for weeks. Then everybody treats me like an old woman. I'm all in!"

She tottered off across the intersection, against the red light, full of battle, defying the years.

Ghostly Disillusion

The idea that prehistoric man was a goof, a thick-skulled, shambling, dim-witted half-monster part way down the family tree from the monkeys, must surely be false. Prehistoric man must have been a lot smarter than we are. By all the evidence, he had to survive monstrous enemies and conditions far worse than anything we can imagine today.

Our ancestor, whom we haughtily look down upon from this twentieth-century eminence, outsmarted them all and survived. The ice age, for example, was a problem of survival that makes our present social and political problems appear trivial. Yet prehistoric man figured it out and survived. How about you and me taking heart? How about us abandoning the notion that we are descended from a race of dim-witted cave men and accepting the fairly obvious fact that we must be descended from a race of supermen, who succeeded in surviving conditions that would have unquestionably wiped us, in our present decayed state, right off the face of the earth? If we can accept this theory, we will take heart. We will remember that we come of a noble strain. As we sit here shuddering at the prospect of the atomic and hydrogen bombs, of protracted wars, and political and social upheavals, we must be a sorry spectacle to the ghosts of our prehistoric ancestors, if any are around.

"Who would have thought," sigh the ghosts of prehistoric man, "that after all our struggles, our descendants would turn out to be a tribe of monkeys!"

———— ❊ ————

The Tree Planters

Old Sir William Mulock, late chief justice of Ontario, who died in his hundredth year, told me that the best thing he did in his life was plant several thousand trees.

"You compliment me on my age," he said. "Do you realize that I will be a hundred years dead before some of the walnut trees I have planted will be ready to harvest?"

Sir William, in his infancy in Toronto, was dandled on the knees of several people who had been born before the French Revolution. It will be 2058 A.D. across what abysses of history none of us can imagine, before the walnut trees will be cut. Old Sir Bill's triumphant glitter of the eye, as he mentioned these things, indicated his satisfaction in the vast span of the centuries he personally had touched.

Out fox hunting, not ahorse but afoot, I came on a farmer in his woodlot, digging a trench in the half-frozen ground

120

around a fine-looking young pine tree about six feet high. The trench, three feet deep, encircled the butt of the tree three feet out.

"When the ground freezes," he explained, "I will come and hoist it out, roots and all in a solid ball, and replant it where it can be seen from the house."

"Why not get the pine seedlings from the government?" I asked.

"This will be a personal tree," said the farmer, smiling, "for my grandson to see. My daughter is expecting."

Sentimental men as well as men with a sense of history are the tree planters.

Turnabout

Two tall grave young men carrying briefcases were admitted to my house by the ladies, under the impression that they were a couple of biologists I was expecting to brief me about a visit they had recently made to Cape Henrietta Maria.

When I went down to greet them, it turned out they were members of one of those religious persuasions which require of their adherents a regular quota of door-to-door missionary work.

But they were such presentable and serious young men in their late twenties or early thirties that I had not the heart to turn them out.

But I did explain to them, before they could unlatch their briefcases, that they could not hold their own faith any higher than I held mine.

Since they, with the utmost earnestness, expressed the wish to state their case, I said I would make a deal with them.

"I will sit and listen to you," I proposed, "for fifteen minutes if, on the conclusion of that time, you will sit for fifteen minutes, while I propound my faith to you."

This was hardly covered by the terms of reference of their religion, and they were slightly baffled. But finally they agreed. I sat reverently for fifteen minutes, a congregation of one, while they expounded. They sat, squirming a little, for fifteen minutes while I made my pitch.

Then we had a cup of tea, and they went on their way, rejoicing. And I went back upstairs rejoicing to my typewriter.

And neither of us was budged an inch.

Logjam in the Cookhouse

Beaverstone Mike was a Ukrainian who brought with him to this country a good deal of the simplicity and innocence that had characterized the village from which he came as a boy. Like most of his countrymen, he did not dally in cities and towns, but headed straight for the frontiers of this country to add to the colour and variety of its beautiful fringe.

Beaverstone Mike worked as cook's helper in the lumber camps in winter; and in summer, he chose to be left behind as watchman or caretaker of the camp, all alone, to feed the unemployed horses, raise a few pigs and guard the stores. The sagas and yarns about Beaverstone Mike are slowly building him up into a character fit to join Paul Bunyan.

A fire ranger arrived at Mike's camp one day and was staggered to find the cookhouse and the lonely tables stacked with pies. Fresh pies, stale pies. Dried apple pies, prune pies, pumpkin pies. On the shelves, pies. On the benches, pies.

"Is the gang coming?" asked the startled ranger.

"No," said Beaverstone Mike mildly.

"But," gasped the ranger, "why all the pies?"

"Different pies," explained Beaverstone Mike calmly. "Some days, I like apple pie. So I make apple pie. Pretty soon, I get tired of apple pie. I think I like prune pie. Pretty soon, I get tired of prune pie. So I make pumpkin pie."

"But holy smoke," cried the ranger, "why so many pies? Look! Pies all over the place."

"I know," agreed Beaverstone Mike firmly. "The cook teach me how to make twenty pies. I gotta make twenty pies...."

"Each time?" enquired the ranger weakly.

"Sure," reasoned Beaverstone Mike.

———— ❊ ————

Prime Time Dropout

During the mucky season of spring, our little dog, a Welsh corgi, has to come in the side door, over some newspapers spread hastily, and go down cellar for a little while to dry off. We have a blanket spread for her down there for her comfort. But she has regarded the cellar as a place of banishment during the four years of her life, having failed to get it through her otherwise shrewd brain that muddiness is a sin.

Just within the past few weeks, as soon as dinner is over and the family groups itself around the living-room to watch TV, Miss Corgi quietly disappears. We did not notice her absence for a few evenings. Normally, she lies in a cool corner under the silent piano, and sleeps through the entertainment.

"Hello, where's the dog?" enquired somebody.

We looked in the kitchen. We called upstairs. We hastily opened the doors to see if she had got outside in the mud.

She was down cellar, in that place of banishment, asleep on her blanket there. And there she goes every night, as soon as TV is turned on, and now even in the afternoons if anybody ignites the box.

Banishment is preferable to what the rest of us put up with.

The Block

On a social service body on which I helped serve as a publicity adviser, we tried every dodge to persuade one of our shrewdest and wealthiest members to serve on a finance committee whose chief function was to high-jack large Canadian corporations into contributing fairly lavishly to the funds.

Two years in succession we failed. He was balkier than a mule. Finally, in desperation, three of us called at his office.

"I'll tell you," he declared helplessly, "why I won't serve on that committee. I won't serve on it as long as Smith serves on it!"

Smith, which of course isn't the real name, is another shrewd and wealthy man who has been on the finance committee for four years, and is invaluable.

"Why not?" we asked levelly.

"Because," said our tycoon, "he is a tightwad, a mean, herring-gutted, parsimonious ..."

This scandalized us because everybody knows Smith has been a most generous benefactor of many causes for years past.

"Look!" said our tycoon. "He wears the same suit of clothes for years. He wears the same shirt. The same tie. By heavens, he wears the same old shoes, year after year. I don't mind a man of means being plain and homely. But he carries it to ridiculous extremes. It gets on my nerves. The same suit, the same shirt, the exact same tie."

One of us, who knows Smith better than most, started to laugh.

"Smith," he said, "buys six suits at the same time, all identical. He buys three dozen shirts, three dozen ties, all the same. He buys a dozen pairs of identical shoes. He hates shopping. He finds what he likes, and sticks to it. His house is full of clothes, but they're all the same."

"Oh," said the tycoon, pausing and reflecting. "I never thought of that."

I mention this story to show that some of our big shots are just as dumb, cantankerous and given to small, pesky prejudices as the rest of us.

Unlonely Silence

My young daughter, on a pre-season visit to the summer cottage, sat on the verandah gazing at the serene and undisturbed scene, and came up with an interesting reflection.

"It's funny," she said. "Nobody else is up here. All the other cottages are closed, boarded up. There isn't a sound. Yet I am not as lonely now as I will be next month when everybody's here!"

"How do you make that out?" I checked.

"When everybody is here," she explained, "I think of all the things that are going on, and I am not in it. All the cottages giving out sounds of people, laughter, yells, calls, children busy, kids swimming, everybody happy. And all I can do is what I happen to be doing. I would like to be in it all."

That is youth for you, wanting to be in it all, and lonely amidst the multitude. But at the same time, there is in this reflection some wisdom as regards the loneliness of cities and the peace of mind to be found in the unpeopled country. City people are always marvelling at the happiness and contentment of those who live on isolated farms or anywhere removed from the crowds and bustle of cities. It is only when we see the activity of others that we become conscious of our own inactivity. Farmers tell me that it is a very uncomfortable feeling business to be sitting idle on your porch when you can see, across the fields, your neighbour ploughing. The happiest, though not likely the most prosperous farmer, is the one whose porch faces in such a way that he can't see any of his neighbours.

In cities are all the materials of loneliness. Crowding about on every side are activities and interests in which you cannot share. Around you are a thousand houses filled with life and drama, but the doors are shut, and the curtains drawn.

Monsieur Murphy

In Algiers, I grew tired of French cooking. Being married to a blonde who talks baby talk must have the same effect on a man as has French cooking, if he has not been born to it.

What I craved was something like thick Canadian pancakes, not the flimsy French wafers you could never dignify with the name flapjack. Corn on the cob. Ham and eggs. A French chef cannot leave ham and eggs alone. He must do something about them. It seems to me certain foods should come, as it were, from the hand of God.

In Algiers, I walked eastward from the smart Europeanized modern section until I reached the district where the French and the Arab began to make contact and blend. I was looking for an Arab restaurant that might invite foreigners. Imagine my delight when I saw, over a small unpretentious shop the sign: Café Murphy.

Murphy it was. Not a doubt of it. I fairly sprang like a flea across the street and peered inside. Corned beef and cabbage with boiled potatoes was my dish, I felt certain. But my first glance revealed that the café was definitely Arab. Inside were Arabs of all shades, from old ivory to jet black. What emboldened me to enter, anyway, in search of corned beef, was the sight of one Frenchman eating pilaf, which is rice blended with lamb or fish or shrimps or some such comestible.

An Arab waiter drifted over to me where I sat.

"Is Monsieur Murphy in?" I requested in my best Chicoutimi.

The waiter, obviously delighted, retired to summon Monsieur Murphy.

He came out in his white coat, wearing a white cloth on his head, turban wise, in place of a chef's hat. Mr. Murphy was black. He was one hundred per cent Africa.

In response to my enquiries, he explained that his great-great grandfather, an Irishman named Murphy, had been captured at sea by the Algerian pirates, and, being a cosmopolitan seafaring man, had settled and become an Arab. I allowed Mr. Murphy to select my meal for me from the Arabic menu. It was a pilaf, and the meat in it appeared to be human ears. Probably some sort of seafood; but not corned beef and cabbage. My next meal was French: *jambon avec oeufs*.

Mitigating Circumstances

An old war comrade of mine who has had a wonderful success in life is bedevilled with a son who is a good deal less than worthless. He has been a constant expense. If you could appraise the value of a son in dollars, I would say this boy is a debit of about $150,000, which, at five per cent, would bring in $7,500 per annum. And at a conservative estimate, that is about what this youth has cost his father for the past four or five years.

Sports cars, trips to England, Bermuda, two different colleges at which he has failed, debts, scandals to hush up, shenanigans, mixups – I think $15,000 a year would be more like it.

How a man who can organize his life in business, in society and in heroic service to his country in war, leading and directing all the way, choosing his men with unerring eye, being iron when need be, can put up with a son who, from boyhood, demonstrated all the characteristics of a lout is one of the most engrossing aspects of the mystery of human nature. The father has not been without advice from his many friends and confidants. I myself on suitable occasions have asked him why he doesn't crack down on the boy. The man who has never in thirty years been at a loss for the right answer to almost any question put to him just stares off into space with a baffled expression.

Recently, the boy got into a jam that was without a redeeming feature; it involved the police, newspaper notoriety, and humiliation. Three of us, old cronies, constituted ourselves a committee to call on our old comrade to see what we could do.

We talked the whole situation over. And we got nowhere. To our astonishment, the father resented our attitude towards the boy. He kept referring to mitigating circumstances.

"What are the mitigating circumstances?" one of us asked.

"You wouldn't understand them," said the father.

"But what are they?"

"He is my son," said the father.

How do you respond to that?

Bright Memories of Bad Moments

It's the fish that gets away that is most talked about.

We spend our lives avoiding misadventure. But it is the misadventures of our lives that make up not only the bulk of our memory but the clearest and best pictures in that mental album.

Last evening, a friend of mine recalled a canoe trip we took ten years ago. And it was with a sense of astonishment that I dug out my recollections of it the way you might grope in the dark for something in a cluttered drawer. I had not thought of that canoe trip once in the ten years past.

After reflecting, I have decided that the reason that trip has all but vanished from my ken is that it was a perfect canoe trip. The weather was sublime. We got fish without the slightest delay or trouble. All our plans were thorough, and everything went according to plan. We had a perfectly beautiful time. In other words, not a darn thing happened on that canoe trip. It was a complete dud. As far as my life is concerned, ten days of it were completely wasted.

In contrast, there is another canoe trip I made nearly thirty years ago. Every detail of it stands out like a painting. It belongs to me, every hour of it. The weather was awful. Every camp we pitched in the rain. Our food gave out. We got lost. All our plans miscarried. We were miserable, anxious, and quarrelsome. But every one of the few fish we caught I can remember to the very colour of its speckles. I can almost heft those fish in my hand. One got away. I bet he was five pounds if he was an ounce. Look: I even had my hand, like this, under his gills....

It's a queer thing: to be precious, in memory, things have to go wrong.

<hr />

The Voices of Noon

No acoustic sound-proofing for the walls and ceilings of restaurants has been found to defeat the noise made by those unfortunates born with bumble-bee voices.

In fact, sound-proofing only seems to intensify the penetrating quality of their vocal vibrations. The average voices are dulled and almost stilled. The bumble-bee voice then dominates the room and irritates all within hearing. A good lunch can be ruined by it.

The owner of a bumble-bee voice is generally a continuous talker. His table conversation is usually narrative. And mostly of a business nature, having to do with thousands of dollars and he said this and I said that. The luncheon companion of a bumble-bee voice as a rule just nods and goes on chewing.

People with bumble-bee voices appear mostly to be short-sighted. They interpret the irritated side-glances of the people at neighbouring tables to be appreciative and interested. The more head-turning, the louder the bumble-bee buzzes. Gosh, what a relief when old bumble-bee tosses aside his table napkin and pats the waitress good-bye!

Next to the bumble-bee, the worst voice is the blatting or trombone voice. A reasonable suspicion may be entertained that the trombone voice blatting in a restaurant belongs to a naturally shy man who has taken courses in public speaking and salesmanship. For if you listen to him, you will hear he is reciting platitudes and slogans. A shy man, who learns not to give a damn is a terrible problem. The more people stare, the happier he is in his sense of liberation from shyness. So he blats.

My voice is like cinders sliding down a rusty galvanized chute. Some of my lunchtime companions say they prefer bees and trumpets.

Long-distance Chirp

When you consider that there is a song sparrow resident during all spring, summer, and fall on every two or three acres of land all the way across America from Cape Cod to Alaska, there should be little wonder on our part how the birds can foretell the weather.

When a song sparrow on Cape Hatteras chirps a warning of a Hurricane Katy coming in off the Atlantic, how long do you suppose it would take for that message, picked up and chirped instantly on its way by the endless chain of song sparrows across the vast continent, to reach, say, New York or Chicago, Montreal, Winnipeg, or even Vancouver?

It is probable that the birds had a means of rapid, almost telegraphic communication thousands of years before man had. Science has no knowledge yet of the language of birds. With regard to the song sparrow, which is only one of hundreds of species, any of which might be nature's telegrapher, it has its well-known and loved song, but it also has a variety of chips and chirps, which are variously called its alarm note, calling signal. It is not at all fanciful to suppose that the birds have special calls with respect to special circumstances, such as the weather, and that a bird sitting on a tree top, is listening to weather reports from its neighbours in all four quarters of the compass, knowing that it is fine in one direction and foul in another, and by the nature of the messages being transmitted, what weather is coming his way.

The theories we have so far worked out with regard to migration of birds, leave a lot to be explained. But if, from several hundred miles east or west, a message is passed in a matter of half an hour or an hour that a fine southerly breeze is blowing and that the senders are already on their way, then we can understand how birds can take off into what appears to be the most unpropitious weather conditions to make their way south. For they know, from the acre-to-acre,

138

mile-to-mile messages of the avian world, what weather conditions lie ahead.

Maybe all nature save man can understand the languages of other creatures. Perhaps there are special harbingers, especially among the birds, to whom all nature listens for news of far away.

Stop Horsing Around

In Hamilton, Ontario, a magistrate had to dispose of a case in which a wrestler was accused of having hit a lady spectator with the flat of a shovel. Apparently it was one of those occasions in which a wrestler is flung from the ring and goes a little berserk on the sidelines. The magistrate, in disposing of the matter, said it was probably a case of horseplay carried a little too far, and he blamed the promoters more than the wrestler.

Now, this is all very well, except for one thing. We horse lovers suspect there is a slight disparagement of horses in this remark. Who ever saw horses behaving the way wrestlers behave, in private, let alone in public? I submit that I have never seen a horse that looked like a wrestler in my whole life. Even those great big fat horses you see at horse shows, jouncing around the show ring with their manes all braided and with ribbons in their tails, don't look like wrestlers.

It is true, the horse, after thousands of years of noble and ignoble service to mankind, faithful unto death and the glue factory or the dog meat factory, is on his way out. But that is all the more reason we should not submit him to contumely, and compare him to a wrestler. Let us re-adapt the phrase, and refer to the larger, lumpier shenanigans of mankind as "wrestler-play."

━━━━◦❀◦━━━━

Principles

"It isn't the money: it's the principle of the thing . . . ." Whenever you hear this statement, smile. For nine hundred and ninety-nine times out of about fifty, you are entitled to smile. A shrewd old family lawyer of my acquaintance has made this statement about money and principles one of his life-long hobbies. Whenever he hears it, he either doubles or cuts in half the money, to observe principles vanish into thin air.

For instance, if one of his clients refuses to pay somebody $100 because of the principles involved, the lawyer arranges a settlement for $50, and then observes the alacrity with which the client pays up.

But on the other hand, where a client refuses to accept $100 on a matter of principle, the lawyer rigs it to have the offer increased to $200. And that settles it.

Now this old lawyer is not cynical. He does not claim that principles are for sale. He merely doubts that the average human being's principles are very deep-rooted.

"Principles are a growth," he says. "They are planted and nurtured by education, training and up-bringing. They are not inserted, like a false tooth or a bone graft. They have to grow into a man's or woman's nature. And being growths, they have to take root. And everything depends on the character of the soil in which the roots strike.

"In fifty years of law practice, I have encountered only two people who allowed their principles to ruin them. And not twenty more who carried their principles so far that they did them serious injury. But in the same fifty years, I have not met twenty others who did not believe that their principles governed their every act."

Out in Front

In the uppity circles among which formless music, shapeless art, and meaningless poetry are earnestly discussed, they use the words "*avant-garde*" to describe those poets, artists and musicians who produced these goods that are so far over the heads of the multitude of us.

As an old soldier, I can't help but resent the employment of these proud words. *Avant-garde* means vanguard or advanced guard, the main unit of a military force that goes ahead of the whole enterprise, the elite of the expedition, first to contact the enemy, and responsible in the fullest sense for the security of all who follow. *Avant-garde* is a precious title, not to be usurped by anybody who likes to fancy he is out in front.

Prospector would be a better word for these intellectuals. A prospector can be a highly trained and skilled geologist, or he can be some old hillbilly with a pick, or even a schoolboy impressing himself and his juvenile circle by going on his holidays with a government pamphlet and a $4 prospector's pick.

In their different ways, they illustrate the activities of these intellectuals, who go exploring out into what we might call the Crown Lands of the human mind and soul. To let these enthusiasts get away with the title of *avant-garde*, however, has an element of the absurd in it. They are guarding nothing of what is back of them; the contrary, perhaps, for they have derision, if not contempt for what has been done in their line in the past. Maybe if they call themselves prospectors, the prospectors will object.

Power (with no sugar) to the People

Democracy is one of those elastic words that, like a Chinese straw hat, will fit any head. Even the smaller dictionaries give seven definitions of it. But apart from that, those of us who use it do not quite know what we mean by it. It is a nice, kind, obliging word. A comfortable, wrap-around word.

Except, of course, in the mouths of our enemies. What they mean by democracy is still more obscure than our own conception of it. Surely they cannot mean it in the sense of number one in the dictionaries: "government in which the supreme power is vested in the people and exercised by them or by their elected agents under a free electoral system."

Even we don't mean exactly that when we fling the word about. We may have in mind number five in the dictionaries: "political or social equality; democratic spirit." But it is more than that. In the democratic world, we are free to be undemocratic if we like. See.

What democracy will mean in another fifty years will be what we make it mean. In 1862, our American cousins were just as certain of their democratic spirit as they are today. But in a book printed that year by Robert Barnwell Roosevelt, uncle of the first Roosevelt president, Theodore, entitled *Game Fish of the Northern United States and the British Provinces*, that estimable and democratic gentleman gives a chapter on how to go camping and what to take along for comfort.

He submits that two gentlemen going fishing should hire five guides. For the gentlemen he provides a fine Sibley tent, the details of which he gives at great length. For the men, as he calls them, a strip of canvas twelve feet long will suffice. The grub list is magnificent. It concludes: "Eight pounds of brown sugar, the same of butter, and two gallons of molasses is sufficient for two anglers and five men. It is not customary to give the men milk, sugar or coffee; they are carried for the gentlemen, and all the above calculations are made on that footing."

The idea of democracy, you see, expands.

A Dog of Character

Among the weird experiments they conducted in Nevada with the series of atomic explosions was an enquiry into the question as to which breed of dog was least affected by fission and its consequences. And apparently the beagle won, hands down. This is no surprise to the several thousand Canadian beagle lovers and the several ten thousand in the United States.

Other types of dog were sent berserk by the explosions, or rendered numb. The beagle was not even impressed by this, the latest of man's wonders. When the explosions were over and the experimenters arrived at the test kennels, the beagles were on their feet, grave eyes alert, tails wagging, saying, "Okay, when do we hunt?"

Nothing excites a beagle but the scent of hare or rabbit. True, he can be induced to be interested in fox or even deer. He is a most obliging small gentleman. But it is the hare that truly excites him. Until he is taken to the fields and let out of the car for a hunt, a beagle is a quiet, dignified, rather reserved and melancholy little hound with little real resemblance, in temperament or character, to his larger cousins the foxhound or deerhound or coonhound. They are yowling and argumentative members of the hound family. The beagle is a bit of a Tory. He is ready for a little fun at any time, but within reason. He will be friendly, affectionate, in a reserved sort of way. But his heart is in the Highlands, or at any rate in the nearest hills where the hare might run. You own a beagle for three years. You know him better than you know your own brother. You kennel him and feed him and fondle him for three years. You are friends.

Then you take him out to the swamp or pasture and let him loose. He finds a hare. Away he goes. He goes by the hour, using his small voice as nobly as he can. And sometimes a beagle can develop a noble voice. The hours wear on. He holds to the line. The hours fade into dusk. You can shout and blow horns as you like. But the beagle stays on the line. So you light a lantern and go into the swamp or out over the meadow, and, placing yourself on the path of the hare, intercept and seize your friend of three years, your chum, your darling. And as you grab him, he fights like a fury with you, you stranger, you interloper, coming between him and his game. After a moment, writhing and wriggling in your arms, he remembers you. Remembers you at last.

A beagle, the fissionists have discovered, is a dog of particular character.

Our Mother Tongues, as they Are Spoke

When I was a boy, there were two names associated with lumbering which fascinated me. They were Meggiban and Muffraw.

I never met either Mr. Meggiban or Mr. Muffraw, though they were reported in my neighbourhood any number of times. It was years before I discovered that Mr. Meggiban was the head of the McGibbon Lumber Company, and Mr. Muffraw was really a Mr. Peter Murphy, employed as some sort of boss over the river-driving operations. Nearly all the men employed in the camps were French Canadians, and their pronunciation of McGibbon and Murphy were the accepted thing. Mr. McGibbon always referred to himself as Meggiban, and when Peter Murphy's son, whom I knew as a captain in the first war, received a detachment of reinforcements from the Ottawa Valley who were nearly all French Canadians, he let it be known that his name was Captain Muffraw to them, and in due time he became Captain Muffraw to everybody in the battalion.

In that war, I had several court martial jobs in company with a Major McCorquodale, he being the prosecutor and I the defence, or "friend of the accused." We had to stay for days at a time at rear area billets and hotels, where Major McCorquodale's name aroused enormous interest amongst the French civilians on whom we were billeted. He had to write it out for them, and pronounce it, and they would stare at it in astonishment and struggle to follow his pronunciation. For some reason, it was to them a hilarious name. Mine was easy. They did not call me Captain le Clerc, but Captain Claque, which means Captain Slap. It induced hilarity.

There was something most attractive to English ears in the sound of English being spoken by a Frenchman or Frenchwoman. The expression on our faces as we listen is almost invariably one of pleasure and of interest, we smile and encourage them to talk; whereas we listen a little stiffly to a German or Russian speaking English. On the other hand, a Frenchman listening to an English-speaking person using French wears a grave expression, occasionally wincing. What we do to French must be painful. And when I remember Mr. Meggiban and Mr. Muffraw, I also recollect that the St. Joachim Dam on the Ottawa is always referred to as the Swisha, which is as near as our boys could get to St. Joachim.

And in all courtesy, or perhaps in sheer self-defence, the French Canadians I have met there also refer to it calmly as The Swisha. They prefer that to what we produce when we try St. Joachim in its true sound.

On the ship *Ile De France* one time I had a cabin steward, a dignified Norman who took sharp exception to my pronunciation of the place name Le Havre. I called it, as did tens of thousands of Canadian soldiers, Le Harve, short for Harvey. After his drilling me for fifteen minutes in what sounded to me like "loo AV-rrrr," I finally passed muster; and my cabin steward instructed me to ask him the question I had previously attempted.

"At what time," I asked, "do we arrive at loo AV-rrrrr?"

"At ten o'clock tomorrow morning," replied my steward politely.

"Do we go directly to loo AV-rrr," I pursued, "or do we make any earlier calls?"

"Ah, yes," said the steward. "First we call at Ploo-moot!"

Being Plymouth. Whereupon, we both relaxed and completed the voyage in perfect bilingual harmony.

Response to a Timeless Urge

Various big brains have made fun of us who fish and hunt. The great Dr. Johnson referred to a fishing line as having a hook on one end and a fool on the other. Lord Byron referred to angling as the solitary vice and had some pretty snide things to say about us. Hunters of all kinds have been subjected to criticism from very ancient times, though until comparatively recently, wild game was a very important item in the food supply of the human race everywhere. It still is, in large areas of the world. And the hunters who provided that food supply were highly regarded members of the community. My own grandmother, in her girlhood, saw as much venison as she did beef or pork in cities like Montreal and Toronto, when the backwoods settlers used to bring in game of all kinds, duck, partridge, a variety of shore birds, to sell on the market.

The grounds on which those who do not fish or hunt make fun of us who do are usually derisive. They scoff at us for pitting our wits against those of a duck. When we proudly assert that we have outwitted a trout with a trout fly made of feathers, there are those who cannot help but snicker at us. Smarter than a fish, eh?

Well, it is hard to convey to those who are not attracted to these sports that there is a great deal of skill involved in casting a fly or swinging a gun on a forty-mile-an-hour duck passing by. It is next to impossible to enlighten a man, who prefers to sit on his front porch, with regard to the aesthetic shock of a partridge exploding out of the underbrush, or the sudden bound of a buck from cover, to your right rear, the hardest shot of all. All fishing and hunting consists of shocks, surprises, instant, sudden, in elements with which we are not familiar. Why do so many of us feel attracted to these things? My own theory is that all of us, every living soul today, is the descendant of successful hunters. If our ancestors were not good hunters, they died, and their children with them. In the beginning, before we had conceived farming, we survived only by hunting, three thousand, ten thousand years ago. Therefore, a good many of us inherit still, from those old forebears, the instinct to hunt, and it would be a difficult instinct to eradicate. And maybe not a wise one to eradicate, because it is an essential instinct to our pioneers today, and possibly to our soldiers, when suddenly we need them.

<hr />

Garlic

We elderly gentlemen of my generation have at least three distinctions: we were born in the reign of Queen Victoria, we have seen the birth and revolutionary growth of the automotive age, and we have borne witness to the rise of garlic from a vulgar herb associated with the most poverty-stricken immigrants up to its present status as an herb of high fashion in cuisine, from the hamburger to the breast of capon under glass bell.

When I was a boy, the only time we ever came in contact with garlic was on crowded street cars when some newly arrived Italian or Middle European stood near us, exhaling through his whiskers an extraordinary aroma that spread through the car like a choking fog. All us loyal fried steak eaters and consumers of overdone roast beef recoiled and screwed up our noses in disdain and disgust. Little did we dream that within our lifetime, that odoriferous white cluster of buds would become as sacred to Canadian culinary art as the nutmeg was then. Now you hardly ever see the nutmeg grater that hung alongside the egg-timer on every Canadian kitchen wall. But almost every kitchen has its garlic press.

There still are, of course, Canadians who recoil from garlic. But I am not one of them. Indeed, on a dare, I have chewed a garlic bud, just to be able to say whether it is a better or worse flavour than our beloved native wild onion, which grows in spring alongside all good trout streams, and which, sandwiched between two slices of thickly-buttered fresh bread, makes a snack to be remembered. Remembered, in fact, for about three days, and causing all those with whom you wish to converse to take two paces back, smartly.

Only one thing has gone a little wrong with the garlic fad. The food industry has invented garlic salt, which, to my taste, is a miserable substitute for the real thing, has a curious flavour of its own, and when used instead of fresh garlic, often ruins the food it was intended to enliven. A French cook has told me: "Garlic is at its perfection when it is employed so delicately and skilfully that you never actually detect it."

In making a salad, he chews a garlic bud and then breathes on the inside of the salad bowl before mixing. Ha!

<hr />

The Trinket

A dapper little man in a grey pinstripe suit and grey felt hat was standing at a downtown bus stop, waiting for the bus, when he noticed, on the pavement by the curb, a small glittering trinket, red and white, peering out of the dust.

He was just about to bend down and pick it up when he realized, with a self-conscious start, that there were also cigarette butts on the pavement. Glancing about, he observed all his fellow-citizens hurrying by. They would think, perhaps, that he was a snipe-shooter: one of those unfortunates who hover about picking up butts. He blushed, and eyed the small trinket furtively. A young lad came up and joined him at the bus stop. He too saw the trinket; and picked it up.

The dapper little man saw at once that the trinket was valuable and he took the boy's name and address and offered to help him advertise his find.

The trinket proved to be rubies and diamonds, part of an ornate pendant lost at a downtown party the night before. The boy got a reward of $100.

The dapper little man who told me this story was penniless. Worse than penniless. His pinstripe suit, his clean grey hat, were literally all he owned in the world. The $100 would have been riches to him. He could have paid his room rent for weeks with it.

He had reached the stage where appearances were everything to him. If he had owned $100, he would not have thought twice about stopping in public to pick up a trinket worth $1500. But because he was penniless, he dared not appear to be picking up a cigarette butt. When I slipped him a few dollars for his rent, we agreed:

Only the rich and the bums can scorn appearances.

Defects

A young lady in our circle of friends came to me very confidentially for some elderly advice in the matter of love. Her romance had been the talk of the family, of course, for several months. I thought it was all settled.

"Pop," she said, "I don't know whether I'm in love or not. Really in love."

"It's easy to tell," I assured her.

"I think I love him," she said distractedly. "But there are little things about him that drive me crazy."

"Such as?"

"Well, the way he blows his nose," said my young friend, hesitantly. "You know. He blows it like a trombone. Or a bugle. He makes that awful, trumpeting sound."

"Mmm-hmm, like a whoopy ball," I suggested.

"And another thing," she said. "The way he scratches his neck. You've noticed it? He is always pulling at his collar and scratching his neck. I could scream."

"How long have you been noticing these things?" I checked.

"Oh, right from the first," she admitted. "I thought maybe I would get used to them ..."

"My dear," I adjudicated, "you're not in love. Love, when all is said and done, is a sort of hysteria, a sort of lunacy which nature afflicts people with at the onset of courtship. This mysterious affliction blinds its victims to the defects and faults in the opposite victim. You see nothing but good in each other. If this were not so, hardly anybody would get married. It is only after marriage that you perceive these irritating little defects. And these are solved by good healthy quarrelling."

My young friend stared at me shocked and incredulous.

"You think I should call the whole thing off?" she whispered.

"Certainly," I said. "And tell him why."

About midnight, my phone rang. I got out of bed.

"Oh, Pop," wept my young friend. "I told him. And he said the meanest things about me. The way I bite my lips. The way I twiddle the hair at the back of my neck ..."

"All over, eh?" I condoled.

"We're being married in February," she exulted.

Butterfly

One of my grandsons, age three, has already made some remarkable biological discoveries. On our window-sills we have pots of those small pink begonias which have the careless habit of dropping their flowers on the sill when nobody is looking. One of these small rosy blossoms, which had fallen on its nose, so to speak, its petals still erect, caught my grandson's eye. He climbed onto the chesterfield to observe it more closely.

"Ah," he said. "Butterfly?"

It is five months since he saw a butterfly.

Enquiring, with a glance at me, if it was proper, he reached over and picked the blossom up between fingertip and cautious thumb. He backed down off the chesterfield. No word was spoken. He motioned with head, eye, and hand towards the door leading from the living-room to the side porch. I rose and opened. Stepping out into the wintry afternoon, he held the blossom aloft.

"Butterfly," he said, with no question mark this time.

He liberated it.

It flew off on elfin wings into the sunlight. We both followed it until it vanished. He did not need to look on the ground at his feet.

Neither did I.

Thrift

My late father-in-law, the Rev. James Murray, D.D., never bought a golf ball in his life. He found them.

Being a clergyman, he could not afford to belong to a golf club, even in the modest era of thirty years ago. But he got his golf during the summer, on one of those pasture golf links that flourished around all summer resorts at that time. He was a thoughtful, thrifty man. Where ordinary golfers mark down the lie of their ball after each stroke, and then walk directly and geometrically to it, Dr. Murray would, after marking down his ball, proceed by a circuitous route, taking in all the rough, all the woods edges, all the likely places where less patient men might abandon a ball.

It was astonishing the number he found. As the years went by, his family could not determine whether he got more out of the golf or out of finding balls. In a sense, it befitted him, as a clergyman, to seek in the waste places for these small treasures. The sinful nature of man was reflected in the impatience, the laziness, the want of Christian thrift responsible for the abandonment of these balls. Dr. Murray would spend the evening repainting carefully his day's treasure trove. Reduced to anonymity, they would be cheerfully given to his fellow clergymen of the summer colony. A bribe, perhaps, because a round of golf with Dr. Murray was a slow business.

He never went for a reflective walk along the beach without bearing home some pine knots from the driftwood. Whatever road or path he took, yielded up a few rusty nails, some small salvage . . . .

He was of the last of many generations of thrifty Canadians.

Pie-lid Lifter

Much to my astonishment, lately, I saw a pie-lid lifter. A few years ago, before the restaurant industry had built itself into the marvel of cleanliness and seductivity which it is today, you could see pie-lid lifters all over the place. If there were four of you at a restaurant table, one of you would be a pie-lid lifter.

A pie-lid lifter is one, either lady or gent, who, on having the pie placed on the table, stares at it suspiciously for a moment, leans forward slightly so as to sniff the pie without appearing to do so, and then, taking fork reluctantly in hand, cautiously lifts the lid of the piece of pie and examines what is revealed. Apple pie was and is the most frequent victim of this assault.

Not more than ten, certainly not more than fifteen years ago, a very noticeable percentage of all diners in restaurants were suspicious people. Whatever was put before them, even the food they themselves selected and carried with them to their table in a cafeteria, had to be submitted to a grim scrutiny. Fork in hand, the diner would poke doubtfully at the contents of the plate, pushing a potato this way, a chunk of meat that, until satisfied that no cigar butts, bottle caps, or other extraneous items were included. Goodness knows what these lid lifters, these food pokers expect to find.

The lid lifter I saw of late was not merely a lid lifter. He was a celery dunker. He picked up his celery and studied it intently. Then he pried it apart, and peered down among the branches. Finding no sea serpents or giant squids, he broke the outer branch free and swished it energetically in the extra glass of water he had had the waitress bring him.

It is a great credit to the catering trade that suspicious diners have so nearly vanished from amongst us that one of them excites the liveliest interest in his neighbours without imparting to them the slightest doubt about their own plates.

Mood Music

The threat of war always brings out the dreary songs. There is a popular delusion that soldiers and war are associated with rousing tunes, spirited marches, resounding patriotic airs. But soldiers have a melancholy taste in music.

In the first war, the bands played "Tipperary." But what did the soldiers sing? "There's a Long, Long Trail a-Winding," and "Roses of Picardy." Yowling, moony songs.

And in the second war, when military bands were, by some curious perversity more or less taboo, what were the soldiers' choices? "I'm Dreaming of a White Christmas," and "The White Cliffs of Dover." The kind of songs you can moan through your nose.

Hitler tried to needle his bully boys with the Horst Wessel song. But what did the poor fanatics come up with? "Lili Marlene," surely the most doleful ditty ever conceived.

During the last war, comedians like George Formby used to tour the war zones, giving concerts of their best and most rousing entertainment. The boys would crowd close and laugh and cheer. But the minute the concert was over, they would retreat to the mess tents or the Y-huts and put "The Warsaw Concerto" on the phonograph.

It was astonishing the grip that piece of pseudo-classic symphony had on all the troops. It was an almost invariable feature, as a piano number, with all the touring concert parties. In the night, in the mud, on a winter mountain road heading to Ortona, as the convoys of trucks, in the interminable halts, chugged quietly in neutral, you could hear from the cabs the low, melancholy whistle as the driver gave out with the theme of "The Warsaw Concerto."

Cured

A bad little boy of my acquaintance was recently taken to a psychiatrist. It was the last resort. His parents, his neighbours, his teachers, were at their wits' ends.

His parents, being modern, intelligent people, do not believe in corporal punishment. They believe in sweet reason. The worst punishment they devised for their problem child was confining him to his room, piled high with comic books full of murder, gangsters, detectives, tommy-guns, death rays. There, in durance far from the vile, the little man could lie and dream up fresh devilment.

The psychiatrist advised them to impose less restraint, not more. The bad little boy was to be turned loose, and left to his own free will and devices.

Within a week, he had been badly beaten up by some children in a neighbourhood formerly forbidden to him; a neighbour, catching him stealing grapes in the garden, had clouted him with a scantling on the behind, causing a slight fracture of the terminal vertebra, very painful to a boy not fond of pain; and finally, coming home near midnight from a movie show he had sat through twice, in his new freedom, he was clipped by a motor car, as he dashed across the dark street, and had his arm broken.

At the moment, he is in bed, and glad to be there.

It would appear that psychiatric counsel, in this case, is a new and imposing name for common sense. Since the parents did not believe in spanking the youngster, the psychiatrist merely arranged things so that life itself would apply the corporal punishment.

A sharp slap from a parent has more significance than a punch on the nose from another bad little boy. The flat of the hand is milder on the backside than a scantling. And most parents, on due reflection, would prefer to do the spanking themselves than leave it to a motor car to do.

At the risk of their child's life, it was the parents who were given the dose of psychotherapy.

Grandma's Cookbook

Cookbooks, the kind you can buy in stores, are all very well. But there is nothing you can buy to equal the recipe book of your grandmother. Lucky is the family that has preserved Grandma's recipes.

Sometimes she kept them in a scribbler, sometimes in a tidy note book. Often she stuffed the book full of loose sheets of paper on which were written, in the various calligraphies of her friends, their recipes she got in exchange for some of hers. As the years went by, the recipe book grew scruffier and more dilapidated. When Grandma died, and her daughters gathered round, you might have detected them secretly, anxiously exploring kitchen drawers. They each were trying to pinch Grandma's recipe book.

In the most honest families, the daughters and daughters-in-law frankly and openly came to agreement over the recipe book, and they passed it from one to the other to be copied. But many a family feud exists to this day based on the suspicion that Grandma's recipe book, which mysteriously vanished, is secretly in the possession of one of the family.

Ah! Cookies, the like of which will never again see the light of day. Pies, potato cakes, jellies, mustard pickles – pickles with a tang and a savour that linger as clear and sweet in the memory as Grandma's face.

You can search, until you are exhausted, through a commercial cookbook, amid those terse, almost hieroglyphic prescriptions, and never find the secrets Grandma knew, and set down in her spidery, tall writing.

My Grandma's cookbook brought confusion and frustration upon her daughters and daughters-in-law. All through it, were references to a cup of this, a half-cup of that, a quarter-cup of another. The only daughter who ever made a success of Grandma's recipes was the one who got possession of Grandma's cup. It held pretty close to a pint!

~~~❖~~~

The Pattern of Christmas

Christmas is becoming stereotyped. All across Canada and down into the States, in city, town, and village, you will see the same decorations, the same routine: the Christmas tree, the early-morning distribution of presents, the dinner, the exhausted family draped about the chairs and chesterfields.

This uniformity in the Christmas festivity is probably due as much as anything else to the colour advertisements and mass merchandising over a period of years. When I was a small boy, there was a great variety in the treatment of Christmas on the one street where I visited the homes of my playmates. At my home, we decorated the mantel, where the stockings – ordinary black stockings – hung from tacks. Across the road, they had a Christmas tree, the first I had ever seen. In still another of my chum's homes, the children got oranges, nuts, and a few candies; but the grown-ups gathered in great numbers to a feast, a feature of which was an enormous cut glass bowl from which steam rose; and there was much shouting, screaming, and laughter. I didn't see any gifts.

At the home of another chum, who was a Jew, they seemed to be mourning, and my brother and I had a hard time dragging him over to our house for the noonday celebration, which was entirely and completely for us children. I hardly remember grown-ups getting in the way at all, at Christmas, even at dinner. I think they were behind us, waiting on us.

When we visited my grandmother, in the country, the Christmas proceedings were entirely different, consisting chiefly of a drive to church in a large sleigh, called a carry-all, followed by an enormous dinner, at which there were overwhelming numbers of strangers called aunts and cousins.

Today, you could attend a Christmas celebration anywhere from Texas to Yellowknife and be entirely at home, and know the drill, just as you would at a Rotary Club luncheon.

Or have you escaped?